# RANKING CORRECTIONAL
# PUNISHMENTS

# Ranking Correctional Punishments

## Views from Offenders, Practitioners, and the Public

David C. May

Peter B. Wood

Carolina Academic Press
Durham, North Carolina

Library of Congress Cataloging-in-Publication Data

May, David C., 1966-
Ranking correctional punishments : views from offenders, practitioners, and the public / David C. May, Peter B. Wood.
    p. cm.
Includes bibliographical references.
ISBN 978-1-59460-589-5 (alk. paper)
1. Punishment. 2. Corrections. I. Wood, Peter B. II. Title.
HV8693.M39 2010
364.6--dc22
                              2009049037

Carolina Academic Press
700 Kent Street
Durham, North Carolina 27701
Telephone (919) 489-7486
Fax (919) 493-5668
www.cap-press.com

Printed in the United States of America

# CONTENTS

# LIST OF TABLES

# FOREWORD

*By Michael Tonry*

Systematic thinking about the imposition of punishments in individual criminal cases began late in the eighteenth century with Jeremy Bentham and Immanuel Kant. Kant believed that punishments should be proportioned to the wrongfulness of crimes. An intentional crime signifies a wrong moral choice and punishments should be calibrated to the degree of wrongfulness. Respect for the offender's moral autonomy requires proportionate punishment. Anything more or less is unjust.

Bentham believed punishments should be designed to maximize human happiness and should be calibrated so that the unhappiness avoided as a result of punishment for crime always exceeds the unhappiness produced by the punishment itself. The references to happiness as the goal of punishment ring strangely in contemporary ears, but the basic idea is familiar. Judges in every case should make an individualized cost-benefit determination. Contemplated punishments whose costs—to the offender and others affected—exceed the benefits they could foreseeably accomplish cannot be justified.

Bentham and Kant are often portrayed as embodying polar retributive and utilitarian ways of thinking and theorizing about punishment. It is seldom in our time recalled, however, that they shared a basic and fundamental belief that punishments, however rationalized, should be tailored to the circumstances and characteristics of individual offenders. For very different reasons, both believed that measures of punishment should be subjective, not objective. What mattered was the effect of this punishment on that person, not the effect of this kind of punishment on the average person. Bentham in particular wrote a good bit about the need to subjectivize punishments to the offender's "sensibility."

In this important book about differences in how people experience and characterize punishments, David May and Peter Wood follow a sentencing path that Jeremy Bentham first laid out 200 years ago, but which few have attempted to follow since. Their new work on this old subject became imaginable only from the 1970s onwards when the institutions and ideologies of indeterminate and individualized sentencing began to collapse. For a century before that, judges and corrections officials mostly believed they should in every case try to balance rehabilitative and incapacitative considerations, and sometimes think about deterrence. There was no need to develop general rules. Without general rules linking crime to punishment, the question of whether the same punishment might affect different offenders in different ways did not come up.

Since the 1970s, indeterminate sentencing has been out of vogue. Most jurisdictions have enacted mandatory minimum and truth-in-sentencing laws, or promulgated sentencing guidelines that are meant to establish general, binding rules. A theoretical literature on retributive punishment, or "just deserts," as it is more popularly known, has come into being. That literature, forgetting that Kant himself wanted account taken of the offender's sensibilities (Bentham's term), argues for fairly rigid sentencing rules in which crimes and punishments are objectivized: X years in prison following conviction of crime Y. What this neglects is that criminal code categories are general and broad and often encompass acts of widely divergent degrees of harmfulness, and that punishment categories are likewise broad. The qualitative experience of a year's imprisonment depends both on the prison (super-max, maximum security, or campus-style minimum security; whether it is well or poorly managed, overcrowded, violent or gang-dominated) and the prisoner (young or old, healthy or sick, robust or delicate, claustrophobic or not, mentally stable or not, a gang member or an employed father of four).

Those are the reasons why Norval Morris and I two decades ago began to play with ideas about interchangeability of punishment. As May and Wood note, we assumed a rough scale of punishments ranging from unsupervised probation to lengthy imprisonment. We wanted to devise a scheme that was respectful of ideas about deserved punishment, but also allowed judges to take account of differences between offenses within a single category, and differences between offenders. In particular we wanted to figure out a way to allow judges to choose between different kinds of punishments (prison v. intensive probation v. home confinement) in particular cases.

We tried various devices. One was to create a system of generic "sanction units" with which punishments could be valued. A year's imprisonment might be X units, a month of community service Y units, a fine equal to a day's pay Z units. The sentence might be for A units and the judge could juggle the Xs, Ys, and Zs as he or she believed most appropriate. In the end we decided a punishment unit scheme could never be made workable. University of Pennsylvania law professor Paul Robinson also wrote a few articles on punishment units but nothing emerged from his work either.

Morris and I finally decided that the best we could do was to propose a general scheme of rough interchangeability and urge developers of sentencing guidelines to authorize use of prison terms or other kinds of punishments as alternatives for particular categories of offenses and offenders. A few jurisdictions, most extensively North Carolina and Pennsylvania, did that. Most guidelines systems, trapped in the view that only prison counts as a serious punishment, did not or did so only a little.

The fundamental problem is that American political and popular culture is remarkably harsh in relation to convicted offenders. For most non-trivial crimes, most people, including most practitioners, believe that only prison counts and that almost all other punishments are less severe. Sometimes the lesser severity is described as inherent ("I'd be happy to spend six months at home sleeping late and watching TV on 'house arrest' "); sometimes it is a consequence of skepticism that state bureaucracies have the capacity or the will to administer seemingly intrusive punishments. Whatever the reason, it is difficult to devise a system for the United States (as occurs in many European countries) in which a week's community service is regarded as equivalent to a month's imprisonment, or a fine equal to a day's net pay is regarded as equivalent to a day in jail.

May and Wood's observation that people have different views about the severity of particular punishments is not new. It is implicit in Bentham's idea that punishments be individualized to take account of individual offender's sensibilities. And it was a frequent finding in evaluations of "intermediate sanctions" in the 1980s: some offenders eligible for a community penalty in lieu of imprisonment always declined, preferring to serve their time and be done with it. They preferred not to be hassled by intrusive and sometimes demeaning conditions and risk failing on the community punishment and winding up in prison at day's end anyway.

What is new and important in May and Wood's work are the efforts to systematically see how groups of people differ in their views about the seriousness of particular punishments, and the findings that there are systematic difference between men and women, blacks and whites, and presumably between and within many other groups. Bentham and Kant would have applauded, as would Norval Morris were he alive, and as I do. This is an important work that picks up threads that others dropped.

# Ranking Correctional Punishments

# CHAPTER 1

# INTRODUCTION TO A THEORY OF SANCTION SEVERITY

In 1990, Norval Morris and Michael Tonry published a modest volume titled *Between Prison and Probation: Intermediate Punishments in a Rational Sentencing System*. This work received significant attention by explicitly promoting a continuum of correctional sanctions to be used in the punishment of criminal offenders adjudicated by our courts. The central premise was that not all crimes or criminals required the most punitive of punishments (imprisonment), and that a graduated continuum of punishments was the most "rational" way of distinguishing the sanctions deserved by criminal offenders. They suggested that offenders with minimal criminal histories and the least serious of offenses should be sentenced to community-based sanctions, of which they claimed regular probation was the least severe. They also posited that, as prior record and seriousness of offense increased, offenders should be sentenced to increasingly restrictive and punitive alternative sanctions. At some point, prior record and offense seriousness required the most severe of punishments (imprisonment, in their opinion).

In this work we question at least two assumptions made by Morris and Tonry. The first assumption we question is that prison and probation define the upper and lower boundaries of a continuum of punishments, and second, that a "rational" sentencing system and continuum of sanctions developed by criminal justice researchers and practitioners would find agreement among criminal offenders who perceive, experience, and react to the sanctions proposed in such a system. Put simply, criminal offenders may have an entirely different conception of what is "rational" than do Morris, Tonry, and others. Consequently, the continuum proposed in *Between Prison and Probation* may be only marginally operational among criminal offenders, who by their own responses to our inquiries demonstrate a rationality influenced by personal and vicarious experience with a range of correctional sanctions and immersion in a criminal lifestyle. If offenders don't see imprisonment as the most severe of correctional sanctions, what does this say about the continuum proposed by Morris and Tonry, and what implications does this have for correctional policy and practice, and theories associated with deterrence, rational choice, and offender decision-making?

# The Promise of Alternative Sanctions

A recently released PEW Center for the States report reveals that by the end of 2008, 1 in 31 American adults were under correctional control (i.e., in prison, jail, or some non-custodial sanction). One in 45 was serving a community-based alternative and 1 in 100 was incarcerated, and the U.S. spends approximately $50 billion annually on prisoner control and supervision (PEW, 2009). Over the past 25 years, while the imprisonment binge has received top billing in the media, in policy development, and in budget growth, correctional agencies have also expanded the use of what has variously been referred to as "intermediate sanctions," "alternative sanctions," "intermediate punishments," "alternatives to incarceration," "sentencing alternatives," and a host of other titles. In general, what is being described is a variety of punishments that are believed to fall somewhere along a continuum of severity/onerousness with traditional probation at one extreme and traditional incarceration at the other. Such sanctions may include elements of probation, incarceration, and alternatives to incarceration, and these sanctions may have a variety of purposes, including incapacitation, deterrence, rehabilitation, and desert/retribution.

Alternative sanctions have attained the status of a panacea of sorts for overcrowded and fiscally-challenged state and federal correctional systems. For example, a 1995 NIJ survey asked over 2500 directors of local and state criminal justice agencies to provide specific areas they believed should be priorities for research or evaluation. At local and state levels, jail administrators, judges, prosecutors, public defenders, probation and parole agency directors, and state directors of corrections identified alternative sanctions as the Number 1 priority for research and evaluation (NIJ, 1995).

Alternative sanctions are attractive for several reasons. First, they are believed to reduce prison overcrowding by channeling offenders out of prisons and into community-based alternatives like house arrest, halfway houses, community service, and the like. Second, the level of risk many offenders represent is too much for probation, but not enough for prison, and alternatives pose a likely solution. Third, alternative sanctions are typically less expensive than imprisonment, and their use would promise some relief from rising costs associated with traditional incarceration. Fourth, alternatives presumably offer the offender a better chance for rehabilitation, while a prison stay may have a negative impact on the behavior of offenders. Finally, refinement of alternatives would seem to promise the eventual development of a valid continuum of sentencing options. Realizing such a continuum necessitates the development of punishment "equivalencies" between traditional imprisonment and alternative sanctions that allow more discriminating sentencing tailored to individual offenders' needs and risk-levels (Byrne, Lurigio, & Petersilia, 1992; Morris & Tonry, 1990; Petersilia, 1990; National Institute of Justice, 1993).

Despite the popularity of alternatives, evidence exists to challenge their promise, and question the wisdom of reforms that expand community-based programs (Doleschal, 1982). Doleschal notes, "Programs have had a minimal effect on defendants, and judges and prosecutors are using them to widen the net of social control." (Doleschal, 1982, p. 133–34). The problem of "net-widening"—perhaps the most common criticism leveled against community corrections programs—implies that instead of reducing the rate of incarceration, such programs allow the correctional system to expand rapidly, placing an ever larger proportion of the population under some form of state supervision. Rather than serving as alternatives to incarceration, such programs more often become alternatives to release. The charge of net widening was first introduced in the early 1970s in reference to diversion in juvenile justice, and remains a primary concern in the development and implementation of alternative sanctions (Klein, 1979; Lemert, 1971; Schur, 1973).

Recent work also points to the intransigence of the "court community," and the problems policy-makers confront in altering court sentencing behaviors (Ulmer, 1997; Wicharaya, 1995). While reforms are passed in legislative session and imposed on the courts, it is the courts themselves—and the individuals who work there—who have responsibility for implementing them. The principal actors in the court community (judges, prosecutors, and defense counsels) work closely together to determine the outcome of cases, and exercise considerable latitude in selecting what they see as appropriate punishment—thereby diluting the intended consequences of sentencing reforms. There seems no guarantee, then, that alternatives endorsed by legislatures will be effectively implemented at the local level (Ulmer, 1997; Wicharaya, 1995).

Perhaps of greater concern, however, are stories of offenders who—while serving a community-based punishment—commit additional crimes in the community. Such events draw enormous attention from the media and citizen groups and invariably hinder efforts to expand community corrections programs. Nevertheless, the search for answers to prison overcrowding, rocketing correctional budgets, and crime control has pushed alternative sanctions to the forefront of correctional policy, and every state has implemented some of the alternatives examined here.

As mentioned earlier, virtually all descriptions of intermediate sanctions suggest they fall along a continuum of severity somewhere between simple probation and imprisonment and that they are necessary to develop a broader range of punishments aimed toward proportionate justice (Morris & Tonry, 1990; Petersen & Palumbo, 1997; von Hirsch & Ashworth, 1992; NIJ, 1995; NIJ, 1993). Indeed, the public, state and federal legislators, academics, and many criminal justice practitioners adhere to the conventional wisdom that probation and incarceration define the extremes of this continuum. Despite this widespread belief, there is a growing body of work that suggests this vision of a sentencing continuum may be severely flawed (Crouch, 1993; May & Wood, 2003; Petersilia, 1990; Petersilia & Deschenes, 1994a, 1994b; Spelman, 1995; Wood & Grasmick, 1999). In 1990, Morris and Tonry urged state and federal authorities to work toward reliable punishment equivalencies and to develop a continuum of criminal justice punishments, a charge that was widely supported in the criminal justice community. However, though justice researchers and practitioners agree that the development of punishment equivalencies is a necessary step toward the construction of a valid continuum of sanctions, few scholars have answered the call to aid policymakers in the development of such a continuum.

# Toward a Theory of Sanction Severity

Gauging the comparative severity of custodial and non-custodial criminal sanctions remains one of the holy grails of correctional policy, and is presumably central to retributive justice. Nevertheless, despite the direct relevance of this issue for the design of correctional systems and implementation of punishments in those systems, it has received limited empirical attention. Traditionally, judgments of the relative severity of sanctions have been relegated to questions of whether to incarcerate and, if so, how much incarceration to impose, under the assumptions that imprisonment is the most severe sanction and its severity is primarily a function of its duration. The proliferation of non-custodial intermediate sanctions, however, raises questions of: a) how to include such sanctions in a comprehensive sentencing system and b) how to evaluate the severity of custodial and non-custodial sanctions relative to one another (Morris & Tonry, 1990; von Hirsch, Wasik, & Greene, 1992). As approximately 70 percent of adjudicated offenders in the U.S. — over 5 million at last count — are currently serving non-custodial sanctions (i.e., regular or intensive probation, community service, electronic monitoring and house arrest, day fines, halfway house), this issue becomes particularly relevant.

In addressing this matter, Andrew von Hirsch and colleagues (1992) called for the development of a theory of sentence severity that not only addresses what is meant by severity, but also attempts to determine factors that influence how a range of sanctions are experienced and ranked. Scholars have used several opinion survey methods to measure the relative severity of correctional sanctions. As von Hirsch et al. note, however, such studies do not address what is meant by severity, nor do they solicit respondents' reasons for their rankings. "It is important that, before adopting the severity rankings indicated in these and similar studies, we clarify, in principle, what should be the basis for comparing penalties. In short, we need a theory of sentence severity" (von Hirsch, 1992, p. 377).

Our work represents incremental progress toward the development of a theory of sentence severity, which has direct relevance for a continuum of correctional punishments that aims to achieve retributive justice and provides a rational scheme whereby sanctions are ranked by punitiveness from the perspectives of the offender. We solicit punishment equivalencies or penal exchange rates from incarcerated offenders, offenders serving probation and parole, criminal justice practitioners (judges and probation/parole officers), and the general public to identify factors that influence the exchange rates between prison and a variety of non-custodial sanctions. We develop scales based on reasons for participating in or avoiding both prison and alternative sanctions, and, using multivariate analyses, we predict variation in exchange rates as a function of demographic, attitudinal, and correctional experience indicators. In this manner, we examine exchange rates between prison and intermediate sanctions and contribute to the eventual development of "... principled interchangeability between prison and non-prison sentences" (Morris & Tonry, 1990, p. 93). It is our intent, therefore, to demonstrate how such exchange rates vary from one offender to the next, and to explore factors that may affect these exchange rates in an aggregate sense. In addition, we explore whether the experience of correctional sanctions influences offenders' perceptions of the certainty and severity of future punishments, and the impact of punishment experience on intentions to re-offend after release. The findings presented here have implications for correctional policy and practice, as well as for theories of deterrence and offender decision-making.

# Offender-Based Research on Sanction Severity

There are at least two approaches that might be employed when ranking the severity of sanctions and establishing "exchange rates" between custodial and non-custodial sanctions (Byrne, 1990). One approach is based on public perceptions of the criminal justice system, which, according to Morris and Tonry (1990), functions primarily to distribute justice in a manner that satisfies the public and allows the public to view such rates as applying a rough equivalence in punishment for "like-situated offenders." Of course, another chief concern of the public in this respect is that punishment strategies control crime and protect communities (Byrne, 1990; Clear, 1994). Such research often uses samples of the uninformed lay public—or "the judgment of the unthinking.... which receives most of its knowledge of the criminal justice system from evening tabloids and television detective programs" (Morris & Tonry, 1990, p. 100).

A second approach attempts to establish exchange rates based on an offender's perspective with emphasis on how offenders perceive and/or experience a range of custodial and non-custodial sanctions. The foundation of this approach lies in the belief that offenders' perspectives are influenced by the length of custodial sentences, as well as by their perception of the conditions accompanying non-custodial sentences and the usual sanctions imposed for failure to comply with the conditions associated with alternative sanctions (Byrne, 1990). It is this second approach that we examine here.

Over the past 20 years, evidence has accumulated that indicates offenders' perceptions of punitiveness or severity of criminal sanctions are more complex than previously assumed (e.g., McClelland & Alpert, 1985; Petersilia, 1990; Spelman, 1995; Wood & Grasmick, 1999: Wood and May, 2003). For example, Hawkins and Alpert (1989) suggest that dissimilar individuals and groups often appraise the severity of the same sanction quite differently; thus, variability in perceptions of sanction severity can translate into variations in the extent to which illegal behavior is actually deterred. Likewise, as noted by Morris and Tonry, "punishments have different impacts on different people" (Hawkins & Alpert, 1990, p. 97).

This growing body of evidence has relevance for theoretical explanations of illegal conduct (e.g., deterrence, rational choice, and social learning perspectives) that operate from the explicit premise that people consider rewards and punishments prior to the commission of crimes. The main implication is that theories need to take into account the issue of exactly how punitive (or rewarding) a given consequence is perceived or experienced by a given individual or by certain groups (i.e., males v. females, first-timers v. experienced cons). Such consequences can include a broad range of responses, both legal/formal and extra-legal/informal, social and non-social. The significance of this topic is not restricted to the realm of theory, as all efforts to control crime are grounded in theoretical presuppositions about why people break the law. Nevertheless, in contrast to Hawkins and Alpert's (1989) notion of relativity, extant policies and practices are more likely to assume an objectivity of punishment seriousness. Indeed, Morris and Tonry (1990) conceptualize the variety of correctional sanctions as forming an objective, calibrated continuum ranging from least (probation) to most (prison) severe, with such things as community service, electronic monitoring, and halfway houses filling the intermediate region.

Work by the Rand Corporation (Petersilia, 1990) has challenged such assumptions by arguing that, given the choice, up to a third of offenders preferred a prison term over intensive probation supervision in the community. Since then, researchers have begun to examine patterns of subgroup variation in perceptions of punitiveness among diverse samples. Subsequently, variation in these perceptions has been found to exist along both demographic and experiential lines (Apospori & Alpert, 1993; Crouch, 1993; May, Wood, Mooney, and Minor, 2005; Petersilia & Deschenes, 1994a, 1994b; Spelman, 1995; Wood & Grasmick, 1999; Wood & May, 2003).

Crouch (1993) and Wood and May (2003) reported that Blacks were more likely than Whites to prefer prison over ostensibly more lenient alternative sanctions. Likewise, Wood, May, and Grasmick (2005) found that males were more likely than females to express preferences for prison over shock incarceration (boot camp). Wood and Grasmick (1999) also observed significant gender differences. Other studies have reported variations by age, marital status, and offense type (Crouch, 1993; Petersilia & Deschenes, 1994a, 1994b; Spelman, 1995). There is also evidence (Apospori & Alpert, 1993; Wood & Grasmick, 1999) that having experienced a given sanction influences subsequent perceptions of the punitiveness of that sanction. Spelman (1995) found that previous incarcerations were associated with a preference for prison over alternatives; it may be that, as McClelland and Alpert (1985, p. 317) observed, arrestees "with large numbers of previous convictions tend to see imprisonment as relatively trivial."

Very few studies have addressed these issues, and the available literature contains a number of gaps in knowledge, including the nature of the relationship between prior sanction experience and perceptions of sanction severity. Important questions that remain largely unanswered include the following: 1) What types of past experiences are important? 2) Do experiential effects vary systematically according to the type of sanction under consideration? 3) What demographic, individual-level, and correctional experience factors condition offenders' perceptions of sentence severity?

Additionally, in comparison to the amount of attention given to the perceived punitiveness of imprisonment in relation to probation, a paucity of work compares prison with so-called "intermediate" sanctions. Since the late 1980s, sanctions such as community service, electronic monitoring, halfway houses, day reporting, and day fines have become increasingly commonplace, even routine in many jurisdictions. It is reasonable to suppose that the routinization of sanctions over time could be linked to changes in perceptions of the severity of certain sanctions, so research updating earlier studies would be useful (e.g., Petersilia & Deschenes, 1994a; Spelman, 1995). Moreover, as Byrne warned over a decade ago, in the absence of more structured tools for decision-making (grounded, we would add, on an empirically valid theory of sentence severity), "judges ... will continue to use ... intermediate sanctions as a net-widening device, while simultaneously expanding the use of regular probation" (1990, p. 29). Additionally, ironies such as offenders being placed on regular probation after being judged "ineligible" for intermediate sanctions due to their level of risk or seriousness continue to exist (Clear & Hardyman, 1990).

An additional shortcoming of the extant literature is that few studies have used samples of offenders serving community-based sanctions (Flory, May, Minor, and Wood, 2006; Spelman, 1995; Wood and May, 2003). Previous studies have used arrestees prior to their sentencing (Apospori & Alpert, 1993; McClelland & Alpert, 1985) or inmates (Crouch, 1993; Petersilia & Deschenes, 1994a, 1994b; Wood & Grasmick, 1999). The lack of research that employs probationer and parolee samples is problematic, given that the vast majority of offenders under criminal justice supervision serve non-custodial sanctions and that threats of other sanctions (such as electronic monitoring orders, halfway house placement, and especially incarceration) are heavily relied upon to induce compliance with probation/parole conditions.

Finally, while Petersilia and Deschenes (1994a) predicted severity rankings by using type of sanction in a logistic regression model, they did not include any demographic, attitudinal, or correctional experience measures and their rankings did not employ a tested system of punishment exchange rates. As such, no previous researchers have used offender samples to regress offender generated exchange rates on correctional experience, attitudinal, demographic, and/or contextual factors in a multivariate model. We do so in our effort toward the development of a valid continuum of sanctions and toward a true theory of sentence severity.

Aside from theoretical or empirical matters, our work has important policy-related implications that should encourage efforts to explore greater application of less costly non-custodial sanctions. If many offenders (or significant categories of them) perceive a variety of intermediate sanctions to be as punitive (or even more punitive) than imprisonment, the claim that prison is the most severe sanction—and a greater potential deterrent—is weakened, as is the primary justification for the continued American imprisonment binge and the huge associated financial costs.

Recognition by practitioners and policy-makers that many offenders perceive certain community-based sanctions as onerous may also: 1) allow a significant number of offenders who would otherwise be sentenced to prison to be placed into community-based sanctions that have a roughly equivalent "punitive bite," and 2) encourage courts to place some offenders who would otherwise be sentenced to token probationary supervision into intermediate sanctions that place more intrusive controls on their behavior (Morris & Tonry, 1990; von Hirsch et al., 1992). Movement toward a theory of sentence severity based on empirical research would provide an organizing framework to support policy-related outcomes of the sort mentioned above, and "would give both the appearance and reality of fairness to the community and to the convicted offender" (Morris & Tonry, 1990, p. 32). We believe our work, which focuses on offender-generated exchange rates and factors that influence those rates, represents an important step in that direction.

# Plan of the Book

In this work, we have compiled and edited several published works that examine punishment exchange rates across a variety of populations relevant to the task. These include offenders serving time in prisons, offenders serving community-based sanctions, criminal court judges, probation and parole offices, and the general public. In each case, we employ a methodology established in Wood and Grasmick (1999) and adapted to subsequent data collection efforts. We detail this methodology in Chapter 2, offer a brief summary of previous efforts to gauge the relative severity of correctional sanctions, and provide a guide that links Chapters 3–7 to the survey populations and data sources used in them. In Chapter 3, we examine punishment "exchange rates" among offender populations, including those incarcerated at the time of data collection as well as those serving non-custodial sanctions. In Chapter 4, we present exchange rates by gender, race, and correctional experience among the offender populations discussed in Chapter 3. We follow that in Chapter 5 by introducing exchange rates from practitioner samples of criminal court judges and probation and parole officers then offer results from a survey of the general public in Chapter 6. In Chapter 7, we explore the possible criminogenic effect of punishment experience on offenders' perceptions of the certainty and severity of future sanctions, as well as on their self-stated likelihood of future crime, and offer a critique of deterrence and rational choice models of habitual offending. Finally, in Chapter 8, we summarize findings from our research on punishment exchange rates, discuss the relevance of our work for correctional policy and practice and for theories of criminal behavior and decision-making, and entertain directions for future research.

## CHAPTER 2

# METHODS OF ESTIMATING
# EXCHANGE RATES

Rather than assume that alternative sanctions necessarily rank above probation and below incarceration in terms of onerousness, one might logically ask if
there are some alternatives that are experienced as more severe than traditional
imprisonment, or possibly less severe than probation. It seems likely that general
agreement exists among inmates regarding the relative punitiveness of a range of
sanctions, but it is by no means clear that the continuum envisioned by policy-
makers mirrors that of prison inmates who know the experience of both prison
and alternatives. Theoretically, intermediate sanctions should fill the gap between probation and traditional incarceration, but in practice this may not be true.
The issue centers on the question of whose opinion determines which sanctions
are more severe than others. More specifically, it bears directly on a "rational" evaluation of costs and benefits by each potential offender, and whether offenders calculate the same costs and benefits in the same fashion as policy-makers.

The development of alternative sanctions—and a rating of their presumed
severity—has been the responsibility of legislators and criminal justice policy-
makers who generally have no reliable means for rating the severity of the sanctions they propose. Punishments devised by legislators and practitioners are
rarely (if ever) based on experiential data, and depend almost exclusively on
guesswork by persons with no direct knowledge of what it is like serving various sanctions (Morris & Tonry, 1990). This is analogous to a film critic rating
a film without seeing it—the readers of the critic's column would be rightly
concerned if the critic had not personally viewed the film. Under these circumstances, the conventional belief that alternative sanctions are bounded by
probation at one extreme and incarceration at the other deserves to be questioned.

Prior to the research efforts presented in this work, only five studies had
examined offenders' opinions regarding the perceived severity of criminal sanctions (Apospori & Alpert, 1993; Crouch, 1993; McClelland & Alpert, 1985;
Petersilia & Deschenes 1994a, 1994b; Spelman, 1995). Three of those five (Petersilia & Deschenes, 1994a, 1994b; Spelman 1995) included a variety of newer

intermediate sanctions in addition to traditional probation and imprisonment. Petersilia and Deschenes (1994a, 1994b) gathered information from 48 male inmates who were primarily non-violent and eligible for participation in an Intensive Community Service program. Spelman examined 128 male offenders, 32 of whom resided in prison at the time (others were serving regular probation, Intensive Supervision Probation, or were in local confinement). Further, the 32 offenders in prison were sampled randomly, and include offenders ineligible for alternative sanctions due to their prior record or the severity of their offenses (Spelman, 1995). Prior to 1999, these two studies represented the entire existing knowledge base of offenders' perceptions of the severity of alternative sanctions compared to traditional incarceration. The methodology outlined in this chapter was conceived out of a concern for the lack of information regarding offenders' viewpoints on alternative sanctions, and builds on the scarce body of work that addressed this issue.

# Measuring Punishment Exchange Rates

Within the past two decades, a number of researchers have attempted to clarify this continuum of sanctions. Spelman (1995) noted that the relative severity of punishments was traditionally measured through three means: comparative judgments, magnitude estimation, and magnitude production through adjustment of comparative judgments. Each of these methods is discussed in detail below.

The comparative judgments method is the simplest of the three methods because researchers using this method present respondents with a series of choices between two punishments and ask which of the two punishments is more severe. If the set of choices is prepared carefully, a rank ordering of all options is possible. As such, a researcher might present a respondent with 10 punishment outcomes ranging from regular probation to incarceration in a medium-security prison. The researcher would then ask the respondent to compare the two punishments (e.g., regular probation v. community service) and estimate which of the two is a more severe punishment. If the respondent rated community service as more severe than probation, then the researcher would rank community service as more punitive than probation and move to the next sanction. By following this method, each respondent could then rank-order the available sanctions by their perceived punitiveness.

A second method, magnitude estimation, involves presenting the respondent with a standard level of punishment (say one year in prison) worth 100 points. The respondent is then asked to assign a score to each of several other punishments compared to the 100 points that are equivalent to one year in prison. In this case punishment perceived as half as severe would receive 50 points, while punishment perceived as more severe would receive a score greater than 100. As Petersilia and Deschenes (1994b) suggest, however, the validity of magnitude estimation depends to a great degree on the mathematical aptitude of the respondents—which is often questionable among inmate populations.

Finally, magnitude production through adjustment of comparative judgments is another technique, but this method works best among sophisticated populations like corporate executives (Keeney & Raiffa, 1976) and is assumed appropriate only for personal interviews due to the amount of explanation and coaching involved. This method has never been used for estimation of punishment scores among offenders, but has proved to be effective in other applications. All three techniques have strengths and weaknesses, but, until recently, most work on punishment severity has employed paired comparisons or magnitude estimation.

# Developing Exchange Rates Measures

In the mid-1990s, one of the authors, with significant input from inmates, helped develop a survey instrument designed to improve upon the aforementioned techniques in estimating the relative punitiveness of prison when compared to alternative sanctions. In May 1995, he spent an afternoon with a focus group of seven inmates in an Oklahoma correctional center to explore the best way of examining the issue of the punitiveness of alternative sanctions compared to prison. Each of these inmates had served previous prison terms and all had experienced one or more alternative sanctions. One inmate admitted experience with five different alternatives. Based on this meeting a draft instrument was developed, and in June 1995, the survey was pretested on 25 other inmates at the same correctional center. After the pretest, the inmates and investigators engaged in intensive discussion about the wording of specific items, the inclusion of reasons for and against participating in alternatives, and the inmates' own experiences with alternative sanctions. Based on the pretest and inmates' comments, the survey was revised.

This extensive consultation with offenders led us to develop a new method that allows inmates to make realistic comparisons based on their own experiences serving time and participating in alternative sanctions. Because all inmates know the experience of imprisonment, and have either experienced the alternative personally or have detailed knowledge of the alternative through the experience of acquaintances, the offender is able to make an "educated" comparison and offer his/her own ratio reflecting the punishment equivalency between imprisonment and the alternative in question. This method allowed a more sophisticated comparison where offenders chose the amount (in months) of an alternative sanction he or she would endure to avoid a specified length of actual imprisonment. The punishment equivalency between imprisonment and the alternative sanction in question has come to be known as that sanction's *exchange rate.*

To determine exchange rates, respondents are presented with descriptions of a number of alternative sanctions, including county jail, boot camp, electronic monitoring, regular probation, community service, day reporting, intensive supervision probation (ISP), intermittent incarceration, halfway house, and day fine. After reading (or being read, depending on the methodology of the research team) the description of the alternative, respondents are asked to consider a set time of medium security imprisonment (generally, 12 months) and are asked to indicate how many months of the alternative they were willing to do to avoid serving 12 months of actual imprisonment. The word actual is often italicized or accentuated in such a manner that the respondent is made aware that the 12 months being considered is 12 months without "good time," which, depending on the state where the data are collected, may reduce that 12 months sanction to as few as six months actual time served in prison.

Using this method, if a respondent is willing to endure only nine months of an alternative sanction to avoid 12 months of imprisonment, then the alternative is viewed as more punitive than prison. If the respondent is willing to serve more than 12 months of the alternative to avoid 12 months of imprisonment, then imprisonment is viewed as more punitive. In this way respondents register their own perceptions of the severity of alternatives compared to 12 months imprisonment, which also allows an indirect ranking of sanctions along a continuum of punitiveness. The actual survey format of the questions used to develop these exchange rates appears in Appendix A.

The exchange rates method provides respondents with a direct and flexible means of comparing alternatives to imprisonment, and indirectly allows a crude ranking of sanctions (including prison) along a continuum of punitiveness/onerousness. Although this ranking is not based on a direct magnitude estimate of the relative punitiveness of sanctions, it is derived from offenders' evaluations of imprisonment and sanctions that they have personally experienced.

The format described above was repeated for a variety of alternative sanctions. The descriptions of sanctions presented in Appendix A appeared in the survey instruments for all results reported in Chapters 3–5. The surveys utilized in these studies also collected detailed background information including age, gender, education, marital status, number and ages of children, and information about the offenders' experience in correctional settings—their longest sentence served, and the total amount of time they have spent in prisons and jails. In all of our data collection efforts, we attempted to include a race identification item. However, one correctional site did not allow us to include the race item. At the time of the Oklahoma-based survey, the Oklahoma Department of Corrections (DOC) was conducting a racial balance study of its inmate population. Oklahoma DOC personnel were concerned that race-specific findings might be politically sensitive, and might discourage some inmates from participating in the survey. Though the inclusion of race-specific findings was of interest to us, we bowed to their request and removed the race item from the instrument. We managed to include this item in subsequent surveys in other locations and Chapter 4 presents race-specific findings. Finally, based on offenders' comments regarding their attitudes toward alternative sanctions, we included items examining reasons why an offender might participate in an alternative and reasons why an offender might avoid participation.

Our primary research questions when we began this work were: 1) How willing are offenders to participate in alternative sanctions, 2) What factors influence offenders' participation in or avoidance of such sanctions, and 3) How do offenders rank the punitiveness of alternative sanctions compared to traditional imprisonment. Throughout our research efforts over the past decade, we have attempted to answer those questions. Each of the samples for which we have developed exchange rates is described in detail below. For ease of tracking, we have included a synopsis of the types of samples that we have used and the chapters in which we discuss those samples in Table 2.1.

Table 2.1  Description of Samples Using Exchange Rates Measures

| Chapter | Sample Type | Location | Year of Data Collection | Sample Size |
|---------|-------------|----------|-------------------------|-------------|
| 3, 4 | Prisoners | Oklahoma | 1995 | 415 |
| 3, 4 | Probationers | Indiana | 2000 | 113 |
| 3, 4 | Probationers/ Parolees | Kentucky | 2003 | 588 |
| 5 | Probation/ Parole Officers | Kentucky | 2004 | 208 |
| 5 | Judges | Kentucky | 2004 | 72 |
| 5 | General Public | Kentucky | 2006 | 1,271 |
| 6 | Prisoners | Mississippi | 2002 | 726 |

In Chapter 3, we begin by discussing the views of Oklahoma prisoners regarding the relative punitiveness of prison. As described above, the instrument that we have subsequently used to examine exchange rates was developed as part of the data collection effort that eventually derived exchange rates from 415 prisoners in Oklahoma in 1995.

In October 1995, a sample of 875 inmates (450 men and 425 women) was drawn from DOC automated files. For inclusion in the sample the offender must have been convicted of a non-violent controlling offense, must not have a history of habitual or violent behavior, and must have received a sentence of five years or less in the Oklahoma correctional system. We used these selection criteria because they roughly identify the population of offenders most likely eligible for some form of alternative sanction, and because inmates meeting these criteria would most likely serve no more than one year actual time in prison. Thus, this group of offenders resembles those most likely to qualify for a range of alternative sanctions.

By the end of 1995 (the year of the survey), there were 17,983 inmates serving time in Oklahoma correctional centers. Approximately 2,800 of these inmates met our selection criteria. Our initial sample of 875 accounts for approximately 31% of these inmates, and approximately 5% of the total inmate population. While the sample consisted of 875 male and female inmates who met our criteria (non-violent controlling offense, no history of violence, and less than a five year sentence), we determined that slightly fewer than 800 inmates were available to participate in the survey. Some had been released by the time the survey was administered, some had been transferred to another institution, and some were serving an administrative sanction and were unable to participate in the survey. Many inmates who were eligible simply refused to participate in the survey as was their right. We concluded data collection with 415 respondents (181 men, 224 women, and 10 who did not report their gender) representing better than a 50% response rate based on those inmates available for participation. This response rate compares very favorably with other voluntary, self-administered surveys conducted in correctional centers (Wood et al., 1997).

The research team met with case managers from eight correction and community correction centers on site in October 1995. Printouts identifying inmates at each facility who met the selection criteria and who had been randomly sampled were distributed to the case managers. Case managers also received detailed instructions regarding administration of the survey, questions to anticipate, and ways to help inmates complete the survey if they required assistance. During October, the survey was administered in classroom settings to small groups of inmates who met the selection criteria, had been randomly sampled, and who voluntarily agreed to participate. All data analysis reported in Chapter 3 is based on an initial sample size of 415 inmates.

In Chapter 4, we examine exchange rates among probationers and parolees. Data from Indiana probationers were collected in the spring of 2000 from a county probation office serving an urban population of about 316,000 in northeast Indiana. To maximize the response rate, we followed a data collection protocol suggested by the chief probation officer. Each week, new probationers were required to attend an orientation session where they had to complete a large amount of paperwork pertaining to the conditions and rules of their probation. The chief probation officer directed the officer in charge of the orientation to administer the survey to the new probationers along with other paperwork.

Prior to distribution of the survey, respondents were assured of confidentiality and anonymity, and informed that their participation was completely voluntary, and that they were free to answer any, all, or none of the questions. Because all of the respondents were new probationers who filled out the survey at the same time as official paperwork, the survey may have been construed as mandatory despite assurances that participation was voluntary. None of the orientation participants declined consent. We concluded data collection with 113 total surveys, including 57 from white respondents and 56 from black respondents.

The instrument used to collect our data was a 12 page questionnaire that included a number of socio-demographic questions and items replicated from Wood and Grasmick's (1999) examination of inmates' perceptions of alternative sanctions discussed in Chapter 3. We collected background information on age, gender, race, education, welfare assistance over the past year, religious affiliation and salience, number and ages of children, whether the respondent had a prior felony conviction, whether their current punishment was for a felony conviction, and whether they were currently serving a sentence due to a drug conviction. We also asked whether the respondent had ever served time in a county jail or previously participated in any of the alternatives examined in the survey.

The second set of data used in Chapter 4 was collected during the fall of 2003 from seven state probation and parole offices in Kentucky. In selecting jurisdictions, we attempted to maximize the distribution of a number of key variables that have previously been identified as important predictors of perceptions of alternative sanctions when compared to prison. As such, in consultation with the Kentucky Department of Corrections, we selected seven districts that would yield large enough proportions of Black, female, and urban offenders to make meaningful comparisons between the groups. Officers in the seven districts supervised approximately a third of the offenders under pa-role and probation supervision in the state at that time. The final sample con-sisted of 612 respondents, which represented 2.3% of the approximately 27,000 offenders on probation and parole in Kentucky at the end of 2003.

On the day of survey administration, a member of the research team arrived at the probation/parole office prior to its opening. In consultation with the su-pervising officer, the researcher was placed in a location designated to insure pri-vacy for the respondent. The supervising officer introduced the researcher to the officers who were meeting with clients that day. The researcher then de-scribed the purpose of the study and asked that all officers send their clients to meet with him/her at the end of the client's scheduled meeting with the officer. The number of offenders available to provide data thus varied based on the as-sistance of the officers in sending their clients to complete the instrument.

After the officer introduced the respondent to the researcher, the researcher provided a letter of consent. This letter: a) explained the purpose of the study; b) informed the respondent that their participation was completely voluntary and that they were free to answer any, all, or none of the questions; c) assured them of the confidential and anonymous nature of the study; and d) asked for the respondent's signature giving informed consent. The researcher then asked respondents whether they would prefer to complete the letter and survey them-selves or have these read to them. Approximately 10% of the respondents asked that the material be read. Less than one in five (19.0 %) of the participants de-clined consent. The 612 respondents included 350 Whites and 238 Blacks.

The instrument used to collect the data was an eight-page questionnaire adapted from the one we used with the Oklahoma prisoners (in Chapter 3) and the Indiana probationers (in Chapter 4) with two minor revisions. At the request of the Kentucky Department of Corrections, we excluded any men-tion of intensive supervision probation and made minimal changes to the de-scription of the county jail sentence. Thus, respondents were presented with a series of questions designed to assess demographic characteristics and the respondent's previous correctional experiences and were also presented with de-scriptions of nine alternative sanctions, including county jail, boot camp, elec-tronic monitoring, regular probation, community service, day reporting, intermittent incarceration, halfway house placement, and day fine. After read-ing (or being read) the description of the alternative, respondents were asked to consider 12 months of medium-security imprisonment and to indicate how many months of the alternative they were willing to serve to avoid 12 months imprisonment. This differed from both the instrument used in Oklahoma and Indiana slightly in that, rather than offering scenarios of 4, 8, and 12-month intervals for imprisonment, we chose to use only 12 months because previous efforts had led us to believe the incremental differences in exchange rates were so slight that it was much more efficient and effective to ask only about 12 months imprisonment as the benchmark to which all alternative sanctions were compared. In some cases, the interviewer was asked to clarify the questions, and interviewers did so following a protocol developed by the lead author. In this manner, respondents registered their own perceptions of the severity of alternatives compared to a year in prison.

We also collected background information on age, gender, race, education, whether the respondent had ever served time in prison, whether they were presently under probationary or parole supervision, and whether they had previously participated in any of the alternatives examined in the survey.

In Chapter 5, we expand the discussion of exchange rates from offender populations to those of their supervisors, criminal justice practitioners. The data analyzed in Chapter 5 were drawn from two sources. The first source of data for exchange rates among criminal justice practitioners was probation and parole officers in the state of Kentucky. In early January 2004, the authors contacted the Department of Corrections (DOC) and asked for permission to administer a questionnaire to officers that was identical to the one previously administered to offenders discussed above. Modifications were made to the demographic portion of the questionnaire (e.g., asking how long officers had been employed in the DOC, asking how many offenders officers supervised) to make the instrument appropriate for officers. With DOC agreement, a modified version of the questionnaire used to obtain data from the offenders was developed to administer to the officers. The DOC contact suggested that the best way to collect data from the officers would be through use of an electronic questionnaire. As such, at the end of January 2004, the authors created a web site where the officers could access and complete the questionnaire. All probation and parole officers in the state of Kentucky were emailed a link to the web site that provided a description of the purpose of the research and a request to participate in the study. After two weeks a second email was sent to remind those who had not yet participated in the data collection of the survey. Finally, four weeks after the initial email and two weeks after the second email reminder, a third email was sent to ask all who had not participated in the research to do so. The questionnaire was removed from the web site in mid-March, 2004, approximately six weeks after the first email was sent to all the officers. Of the 295 officers who supervised clients in the state of Kentucky in January 2004, 208 officers responded, for a participation rate of 70.5%.

The second source of data considered in Chapter 5 comes from judges in the state of Kentucky. Responses from judges were collected via surveys during the fall of 2004 from all the county judges that were currently serving in the state of Kentucky and had presided over a circuit court (or were currently in that role). Of the 132 active judges in the state, 96 presided in a circuit court and 36 in a family court. A list of the names and addresses of all the sitting judges in the state was solicited from the Kentucky Administrative Office of the Courts (AOC) and consequently served as the target sample.

Permission to administer the questionnaires was first solicited from the AOC. Once granted, the surveys were distributed at a state conference where nearly all of the 132 active county judges were expected to attend in the fall of 2004. Despite our request to be involved in the questionnaire administration at the conference, the distribution and collection of the surveys was delegated to an AOC representative who worked in conjunction with the research team. As such, the exact time, method, and manner the instruments were distributed could not be controlled or monitored. Nevertheless, we were able to determine the contents of the packet to be distributed and, in addition to the questionnaire; we included a cover page introducing the study, provided contact information in case of any problems or questions, and insured the respondents of its anonymous nature.

After the completed surveys were returned from the conference, follow-up packets were sent approximately 30 days later to every judge whose name and address was provided by the court administrator contact. The packet contained an introduction letter, the survey, and a pre-stamped return envelope. Approximately two weeks after the initial mailing, a second packet containing the same materials, with some modifications to the cover letter, was mailed out to all judges who had thus far failed to return the initial mailings. A similar third follow-up packet with additional revisions to the cover letter was sent two weeks after the second mailing to all those who have failed to respond. These efforts resulted in responses from 72 judges, a response rate of 54.5%.

In Chapter 6, we discuss the exchange rates we found among the general public. These data were collected from a sample of Kentucky residents in the late spring of 2006. A slightly modified version of the questionnaire used in the previous data collection efforts was sent to 4,000 mailing addresses purchased from a direct mailing firm that insured maximum coverage of Kentucky households. We oversampled in Jefferson County (700 addresses) and Fayette County (300 addresses) because these counties contained the vast majority of African Americans in Kentucky. The remaining 3,000 addresses were randomly distributed throughout the state.

A postcard describing the purpose of the research and informing the respondents of the study was sent to the addresses provided. After two weeks, we cleaned any returned postcard addresses from the sample and mailed the questionnaire with a cover letter describing the purpose of the study and asking the adult who received the letter to participate. After two weeks, we sent a post-card reminder to all addresses that had not returned a questionnaire. Next, four weeks after the original mailing, we sent a packet containing a second copy of the original questionnaire and a revised cover letter again requesting the respondent's participation. Finally, eight weeks after the original cover letter and three weeks after the second packet was sent to the respondents, a third questionnaire (with a revised cover letter) was sent to ask all who had not participated in the research to do so. Of the 4,000 respondents for whom we originally received an address, 380 were determined to be invalid addresses, and 1,313 respondents provided a usable questionnaire. As such, the participation rate was 36.3%.

In Chapter 7, we use data from Mississippi prisoners to attempt to understand differences in exchange rates and the implications for these differences in terms of recidivism. These data were gathered at the central assessment and reception facility in the Mississippi correctional system. The facility is the second largest correctional center in the state and held approximately 3,000 inmates at the time of the survey, including all female inmates in the state system (approximately 1,300 at the time). It is also the entry point for all offenders sentenced to serve time in the state correctional system. We began the data collection by organizing two focus groups — one with eight male inmates and one with eight female inmates—to solicit their input regarding potential factors that might motivate or inhibit re-offending upon release. Based on prior experience working with inmate populations, current knowledge of the extant literature, and comments from focus group participants, a pilot survey was pre-tested on 21 male and 21 female inmates (separately). Immediately following the pre-test, comments were solicited from pre-test participants in open discussion. The survey was again revised based on pilot survey results and inmate comments. The final questionnaire was 11 pages long and required approximately 30 minutes to complete.

Prior to selection of the sample, meetings were held with administrators and wardens from the DOC to determine the best data collection procedure (i.e., the least disruptive method of generating the largest number of respondents). Administrators advised that the optimal procedure would be to have unit managers advertise the data collection effort on the day prior to the arrival of the research team and identify volunteers to participate in the research on the following day.

The final draft of the instrument was administered to samples of male and female inmates in December 2001 and January 2002. The design of the prison was such that there were over 20 housing units of varying security levels dispersed throughout the prison grounds. Inmates were brought to one central meeting space in both the female and male portions of the facility where the study was explained by the research team. Males completed the questionnaire in a large, cafeteria-style room in groups of approximately 100 inmates per session in the male portion of the correctional facility; female inmates were surveyed in groups of 20–30 in a smaller conference room on the women's side of the facility during a series of visits to the institution.

For the purposes of this research, inmates were viewed as "experts" who had knowledge about the prison experience and criminal offending that the research team did not. After the research team explained the study, inmates still interested in participating remained seated, while those not wishing to participate were returned to their respective cells. The remaining inmates were then given a more in-depth explanation of the study and a consent form that provided contact information should any participant wish to learn more about the study. Members of the research team remained in the room to answer questions and to ensure that no interaction occurred between respondents and DOC personnel. For security reasons, two or three correctional employees remained in the room at all times, though they stood at one end of the room and tried to be as unobtrusive as possible.

Given the constraints placed upon the research team by the administrators, it is quite possible that there is some type of selection bias due to the voluntary nature of the study. Nevertheless, it is difficult to determine what kind of selection may have taken place, or if it impacted our results. It is possible that inmates who could not read were discouraged from participating in the self-administered survey. Furthermore, it is also likely that "uncooperative" inmates declined, and that inmates on certain restrictions were unable to participate. Finally, prior experience tells us that some unit administrators probably did not inform the inmates housed in their unit about the data collection each time the researchers were there to collect data.

Given these factors, and others that remain unknown but which are peculiar to that day in that institution, we hesitate to provide a "response rate" because we have no idea how many inmates were actually aware that the survey was being administered and chose not to participate. Nevertheless, the most conservative response rate would be 24% (726 inmate responses divided by the maximum capacity of 3,000), though the true response rate is likely higher. Nevertheless, this sample, however haphazard it may be, is uniquely suited to address issues of imprisonment and decision-making among criminal offenders considered in Chapter 7. Data collection in correctional institutions is fraught with special restrictions and procedures, but we feel that the richness of the data in our sample outweighs concerns about how representative it might be.

# CHAPTER 3

# EXCHANGE RATES AMONG OFFENDER POPULATIONS

Intuitively, the most logical group of respondents to provide data regarding the relative punitiveness of prison is those who have actually experienced the sanction of prison itself. As such, we began our efforts to use exchange rates to determine the relative severity of prison when compared to alternative sanctions with prisoners in Oklahoma. The method through which we collected that data was described in Chapter 2; details about the sample are presented below.

All the inmates were convicted of non-violent controlling offenses and had been sentenced to five years or less for their current offense. Other descriptive information about the inmate respondents is displayed in Table 3.1.

Overall, the inmate respondents had served an average of one year and nine months total time in prisons, with males averaging two years three months and females averaging one year four months. The average duration of their longest single prison stay was about 15 months. The inmates averaged 33 years of age, and just over 11 years education. Nearly 80% of female inmates and 65.7% of males had at least one child. Despite this high rate of parenthood, only 23.4% of males and 19.3% of females were married at the time of the data collection. In sum, the inmates in the study represent the kind of offenders' most likely eligible for participation in a range of alternative sanctions.

## Inmates' Willingness to Participate in Alternative Sanctions

There are several ways to represent the punitiveness of the sanctions examined in this study. We start with the percent of inmate respondents who refused to do any amount of an alternative to avoid 4, 8, or 12-months imprisonment. The percentages of inmate respondents (men and women combined) who refused to participate in the specified sanctions are presented in Table

3.2. As might be expected, the percent of inmates who refused to do any amount of an alternative to avoid imprisonment decreases as the length of actual imprisonment increases.

Table 3.1  Descriptive Statistics of the
Oklahoma Inmate Sample, Men, and Women

|  | Men | Women | All Respondents |
|---|---|---|---|
| Number of Cases[a] | 181 | 224 | 415 |
| Average Age | 34 | 32 | 33 |
| Average Years Education | 11.34 | 11.31 | 11.32 |
| Marital Status: Percentages (Ns) |  |  |  |
| Single, never married | 36.0 (63) | 38.1 (83) | 37.2 (147) |
| Single, divorced, or separated | 39.4 (69) | 37.6 (82) | 38.2 (151) |
| Currently married | 23.4 (41) | 19.3 (42) | 21.0 (83) |
| Widowed (spouse died) | 1.1 (2) | 5.0 (11) | 3.5 (14) |
| R Has at Least One Child | 65.7 (119) | 79.5 (178) | 71.8 (298) |
| Total Time in All Prisons: |  |  |  |
| Median | 2 yrs 3 mo | 1 yr 4 mo | 1 yr 9 mo |
| Longest Single Prison Stay: |  |  |  |
| Median | 1 yr 4 mo | 1 yr 3 mo | 1 yr 3 mo |

[a] Men and women do not add up to 415 because 10 respondents did not state their gender.

Table 3.2  Percentages of Oklahoma Inmates Who Refuse to Participate in the Specified Alternative Sanction to Avoid 4, 8, or 12 Months of Medium-Security Imprisonment (Numbers of Inmates Refusing in Parentheses)

| Alternative Sanction | Months of Actual Imprisonment | | |
|---|---|---|---|
|  | 4 Months | 8 Months | 12 Months |
| County Jail | 28.9 (112) | 20.4 (79) | 19.8 (77) |
| Boot Camp | 29.9 (116) | 23.7 (92) | 23.2 (90) |
| Electronic Monitoring | 21.9 (85) | 14.2 (55) | 14.4 (56) |
| Regular Probation | 20.9 (81) | 14.2 (55) | 12.4 (48) |
| Community Service | 12.6 (49) | 10.1 (39) | 8.8 (34) |
| Day Reporting | 19.6 (76) | 15.2 (59) | 15.7 (61) |
| ISP | 26.3 (102) | 20.4 (79) | 18.8 (73) |
| Intermittent Incarceration | 15.2 (59) | 11.9 (46) | 11.6 (45) |
| Halfway House | 9.3 (36) | 7.0 (27) | 6.7 (26) |
| Day Fine | 28.4 (110) | 24.7 (96) | 24.0 (93) |

Nearly 30% of respondents refused to endure any amount of boot camp to avoid 4 months imprisonment but the percentage dropped to 23.2% in the case of 12 months imprisonment. The least objectionable alternative for this sample was the halfway house, with less than 10% of inmates refusing to enroll in halfway house to avoid four months imprisonment, a figure that drops to 6.7% in the case of 12 months actual time in prison. The data in Table 3.2 indicate that over 20% of inmates refused to enroll in any amount of Boot Camp, County Jail, Day Fines, Intensive Supervision Probation (ISP), Electronic Monitoring, or Regular Probation to avoid just four months actual imprisonment. The results presented in Table 3.2 also suggest that, for many inmates, several alternatives were perceived as more punitive than actual imprisonment, to the point where some inmates would avoid all contact with the alternative even if it means spending less time in prison.

In her study of nonviolent offenders in Oregon, Petersilia (1990) found that nearly one third of offenders given the option of participating in ISP (Intensive Supervision Probation) chose prison instead.

> Offenders evidently felt that going to work every day, being drug tested, and having their home privacy invaded were more punishing than serving a stint in state prison. Not only did they perceive the ISP conditions as onerous but many offenders predicted they would not be able to abide by these conditions, and would eventually be revoked to prison to serve out their original sentence (Petersilia and Deschenes, 1994b, p. 310).

As it turns out, 50% of the offenders participating in Oregon's ISP program were revoked to prison within one year. Similar to findings presented by Petersilia, the results displayed in Table 3.2 indicate that over 26% of inmates in the current study refused to participate in ISP (29.8% of male inmates refused, virtually the same refusal rate noted by Petersilia among the male offenders in her study).

It is clear that a significant proportion of inmates that might be eligible for alternative sanctions want nothing to do with them. This raises the question of what it is about alternative sanctions that attracts inmates to them, or repels inmates from participating in them. This issue generated significant debate and commentary from inmates in both the focus group and the pre-test and led us to include items in the final survey that addressed this point. As such, the reasons for and against participation in alternative sanctions that are presented in Tables 3.3 and 3.4 include many suggested by inmates themselves.

The results presented in Table 3.3 indicate that the most important reasons inmates (men and women combined) choose for participating in alternatives involve obligations or opportunities that exist outside prison. The vast majority

Table 3.3 Reasons Why Oklahoma Inmates Would Participate
in an Alternative Sanction: Percentages[a,b]

| Reasons | Responses | | | |
|---|---|---|---|---|
| | 1 | 2 | 3 | 4 |
| Offender has a job outside prison. | 76.0 | 12.8 | 5.8 | 5.3 |
| Offender has wife/husband outside prison. | 61.3 | 15.3 | 10.9 | 12.4 |
| Offender has children outside prison. | 83.9 | 5.4 | 5.6 | 5.1 |
| Offender is being victimized by other inmates and is doing "hard time." | 30.2 | 19.8 | 26.5 | 23.5 |
| Offender is serving his/her first term in prison. | 56.5 | 21.1 | 14.0 | 8.4 |
| Correctional institution in which the offender is serving time is very strict on inmates. | 24.9 | 23.4 | 25.4 | 26.3 |
| Alternatives offer a better lifestyle than prison. | 58.3 | 17.6 | 12.9 | 11.2 |
| Alternatives allow the inmate to live outside prison. | 71.2 | 14.5 | 7.6 | 6.7 |
| Alternatives have a good reputation among inmates. | 41.5 | 23.2 | 14.8 | 20.5 |
| Alternatives successfully rehabilitate the offender. | 56.7 | 19.5 | 13.3 | 10.6 |
| Offender is a woman. | 30.9 | 12.2 | 18.5 | 38.4 |
| Alternatives are easier to complete than a prison term. | 40.4 | 22.1 | 18.1 | 19.4 |
| Alternatives help you get out of prison sooner. | 63.4 | 15.6 | 11.0 | 10.0 |

[a] We want to know how important you think those reasons are for participating in an alternative sanction. For each reason on the left, circle the number that tells how important you think that reason is for choosing the alternative sanction. 1. Very important reason; 2. Pretty important reason; 3. Somewhat important reason; 4. Not at all important.
[b] N = 415

(83.9%) of inmates said having children outside prison was a very important reason for participating in alternatives and 61.3% cited having a spouse outside prison as very important. Three in four (76%) inmates said having a job waiting for them outside prison was a very important reason for enrolling in alternatives. Other factors include that alternatives allowed the inmate to live outside prison (a very important reason for 71.2% of inmates) and that alternatives helped them get out of prison sooner (very important for 63.4% of inmates).

It seems the onerousness of imprisonment plays only a minor role in inmates' decisions to enroll in alternatives. The least important reason for participating in

Table 3.4  Reasons Why Inmates Would Avoid an
Alternative Sanction: Percentages[a,b]

| Reasons | Responses | | | |
| --- | --- | --- | --- | --- |
| | 1 | 2 | 3 | 4 |
| Programs like those in this survey are too hard to complete. | 24.4 | 21.0 | 24.0 | 30.6 |
| Program rules are too hard to follow. | 23.8 | 24.5 | 22.3 | 29.4 |
| Parole and program officers are too hard on the program participants; they try to catch them and send them back to prison. | 46.8 | 15.8 | 17.3 | 20.1 |
| Serving time in prison is easier than the alternatives offered by the DOC. | 32.6 | 19.8 | 20.0 | 27.7 |
| If you fail to complete the alternative sanction, you end up back in prison. | 57.7 | 15.6 | 13.9 | 12.9 |
| In general, living in prison is easier than living outside prison. | 22.9 | 13.7 | 14.7 | 48.8 |
| Inmates are abused by parole and probation officers who oversee the programs. | 40.5 | 18.5 | 16.3 | 24.7 |
| Serving time in prison is less hassle because the programs have too many responsibilities. | 2.1 | 20.2 | 19.5 | 34.2 |

[a] We want to know how important you think these reasons are for avoiding an alternative sanction like those presented on the survey. For each reason on the left, circle the number that tells how important you think that reason is for avoiding the alternative sanction. 1. Very important reason; 2. Pretty important reason; 3. Somewhat important reason; and 4. Not at all important.
[b] N = 415

alternatives involved the strictness of the correctional institution in which the offender was serving time, with over 26% saying this was not at all important. Likewise, the explanation that the offender was being victimized by other inmates and is doing "hard time" was very important for only 30.2% of inmates and not at all important for 23.5% of inmates. However, it does appear that alternatives are more attractive for offenders serving their first prison term, with 56.5% of inmates saying that was a very important reason for participation. It is possible that, after a period of adaptation and adjustment, inmates may become more amenable to serving prison, and less willing to gamble on alternatives.

While the results in Table 3.3 display reasons why inmates (men and women combined) might participate in alternative sanctions, the results in Table 3.4 shows reasons why inmates would avoid them. The three most important reasons why inmates would avoid alternatives are: 1) "If you fail to complete the alternative sanction, you end up back in prison" (57.7% very important); 2) "Parole and program officers are too hard on the program participants, they try to catch them and send them back to prison" (46.8% very important); and 3) "Inmates are abused by parole and probation officers who oversee the programs" (40.5% very important).

Apparently, the uncertainty of completing the alternative, coupled with the presumed manner in which alternatives are administered by parole and program officers, serve to discourage many inmates from participation, a finding consistent with work by both Petersilia (1990) and Spelman (1995). The common sentiment among inmates was that they would rather serve out their term and be released with no strings attached than invest significant time in an alternative sanction involving potentially abusive program officers and a strong likelihood of failure and revocation. For many inmates, a brief prison term was the lesser of two evils compared to the uncertainty of completing an alternative sanction. Particularly among inmates with more experience in the system, imprisonment becomes familiar, while the outcome of involvement in alternatives becomes less certain and less attractive. Inmates in Spelman's (1995) study of alternative sanctions acknowledged this in the following quotes:

> Probation [ISP] has too many conditions. If you can't meet them, you end up in jail anyway. I'd rather just do the time and pay off my debt to society that way. On probation, you're on a short leash. If you cross over the line, they give you more time. The longer it lasts, the more chances you have to mess up. If you break [probation conditions], you'll do longer than a year in jail (Spelman, 1995, p. 126).

In fact, based on the responses to the questions that asked about the difficulty of the programs, the difficulty of the program rules, and the onerous nature of the program rules, few inmates view the formal rules and responsibilities of the alternatives as a serious obstacle. Based on our findings, it appears that inmates with experience serving time view alternative sanctions less favorably than those serving their first imprisonment.

# The Punitiveness of Alternative Sanctions Compared to Imprisonment

We now turn to the punitiveness of alternative sanctions compared to fixed durations of imprisonment among inmates who have had direct, personal experience with the sanction in question. We feel these are the inmates most knowledgeable about alternatives and it is their opinions that would seem most relevant. Table 3.5 shows the average and median amounts (the median is expressed in terms of the nearest whole number) of the alternative sanction inmates (men and women combined) would do to avoid 4, then 8, then 12-months medium security imprisonment. Again, only inmates with personal experience of that sanction are included—inmates who refused to participate are excluded from Table 3.5. The number of inmates who say they have personal experience with a particular sanction is listed below each sanction.

Table 3.5  Average/Median Amount of Alternative Sanction Inmates Would Be Willing to Serve to Avoid 4, 8, and 12 Months of Medium-Security Imprisonment (Alternative Sanction Unit of Analysis in Parentheses)

| Alternative Sanction | Months of Actual Imprisonment | | |
| --- | --- | --- | --- |
| | 4 | 8 | 12 |
| County Jail (Months) | 2.87/2 | 3.89/4 | 5.02/4 |
| N of cases | (239) | (274) | (281) |
| Boot Camp (Months) | 2.53/2 | 3.65/4 | 4.95/4 |
| N of cases | (111) | (118) | (117) |
| Electronic Monitoring (Months) | 4.64/4 | 7.21/6 | 9.75/8 |
| N of cases | (64) | (70) | (69) |
| Regular Probation (Years) | 2.63/1 | 3.32/2 | 4.18/3 |
| N of cases | (216) | (238) | (245) |
| Community Service (Hours) | 528/250 | 772/500 | 1,160/750 |
| N of cases | (176) | (188) | (191) |
| Day Reporting (Months) | 3.71/4 | 5.68/5 | 6.72/6 |
| N of cases | (24) | (25) | (25) |
| ISP (Months) | 5.37/4 | 7.28/6 | 9.18/6 |
| N of cases | (41) | (47) | (49) |
| Intermittent Incarceration (Days) | 83/60 | 121/90 | 145/120 |
| N of cases | (31) | (32) | (33) |
| Halfway House (Months) | 4.82/4 | 6.91/7 | 8.51/10 |
| N of cases | (108) | (113) | (115) |
| Day Fine (Days) | 127/90 | 151/120 | 171/150 |
| N of cases | (25) | (25) | (26) |

Note:  Only inmates with experience in serving each sanction are included, Inmates who refused to participate are excluded.

In Table 3.5, the numbers represent the unit of analysis listed after each sanction. County Jail, Boot Camp, Electronic Monitoring, Day Reporting, ISP, and Halfway House are measured in terms of months, Intermittent Incarceration and Day Fine are measured in terms of days, and Community Service and Regular Probation are measured in terms of hours and years, respectively. The results presented in Table 3.5 demonstrate that inmates who have experienced County Jail would do an average of 2.87 months of County Jail to avoid serving 4 months of actual imprisonment (N of Cases = 239), an average of 3.89 months to avoid 8 months imprisonment (N = 274), and 5.02 months to avoid 12 months imprisonment (N = 281). Given these crude "equivalencies," one may conclude that inmates who have experienced both sanctions rate County Jail as significantly more punitive than prison. While this may seem strange to those not familiar with serving time, Fleisher (1995) and others have found that offenders would routinely rather do a longer prison term than a short jail sentence.

Similar to County Jail, 111 inmates who had experienced Boot Camp would do an average of 2.53 months of Boot Camp to avoid serving 4 months of actual imprisonment, an average of 3.65 months of Boot Camp to avoid 8 months imprisonment (N = 118), and an average of 4.95 months to avoid 12 months imprisonment (N = 117). The data thus revealed that inmates viewed Boot Camp as significantly more punitive than imprisonment.

On the other hand, the 108 inmates who have experienced Halfway House would do an average of 4.82 months of Halfway House to avoid 4 months imprisonment—indicating that 4 months of imprisonment is more onerous than 4 months of Halfway House. However, this ratio does not hold when one moves to 8 months (N = 113) and then 12 months actual imprisonment (N = 115), with tradeoffs of 6.91 and 8.51 months of Halfway House respectively. For most alternative sanctions, the additional amount of time inmates were willing to invest in the alternative declined as the actual prison stay increased from 4 to 8 to 12-months imprisonment. As such, there was clearly a law of diminishing returns that applied to this phenomenon. Inmates were not willing to do three times as much of the alternative to avoid 12 months imprisonment as they would to avoid 4 months imprisonment. Though the duration of imprisonment was multiplied by three, the amount of the alternatives that inmates were willing to serve rarely exceeded twice the amount they would do to avoid just four months imprisonment. This was likely due to the increased certainty of revocation over a longer period of time.

Inmates who had experienced Regular Probation would do an average of 2.63 years of Probation to avoid 4 months imprisonment (N = 216), 3.32 years of Probation to avoid 8 months imprisonment (N = 238), and 4.18 years of Pro-

bation to avoid 12 months imprisonment (N = 245). Clearly, Regular Probation was viewed as far less punitive than imprisonment and was in fact the
least punitive of all the sanctions rated by inmates in the study. This supports
the claim that traditional probation represents the low end on a continuum of
severity/onerousness of sanctions. However, the claim that traditional imprisonment represents the high end of the severity continuum is challenged
when examining findings presented in Table 3.5.

It is possible to construct a crude ranking of the relative punitiveness of
sanctions based on information presented in Table 3.5. In doing so, we make
some arbitrary (but informed) decisions regarding the calculation of sentence
duration—particularly for sanctions measured in hours or days. In the case
of Community Service, an extremely heavy sentence would involve 20 hours
of service per week. Most offenders do not have such a schedule and usually
do fewer than 20 hours per week. However, we arbitrarily imposed a 20 community hour week—which came to 80 hours per month. We then divided
the total number of hours an inmate would serve by 80 to arrive at the number of months of Community Service the inmate would serve to avoid a specified length of imprisonment. Regarding Intermittent Incarceration, we
presumed a five night/week incarceration sentence (allowing offenders to
spend weekends at home). This amounted to approximately 20 nights per
month. We then divided the total nights an inmate would serve by 20 to get
the number of months he/she would serve to avoid a certain length of imprisonment. Day Fine, which is primarily a monetary sanction and a function
of the income and employment status of the offender, is not included in our
ranking of punitiveness because we lacked that information for each offender.
It should be noted, however, that Day Fine generates perhaps the highest refusal rates in Table 3.4 and was clearly one of the more punitive alternative sanctions in the study.

Using the above calculations, we produced a crude ranking of sanction
severity shown in Table 3.6. Punitiveness rankings in the "4 Months Index"
column in Table 3.6 suggest that imprisonment would rank no higher than fourth
in punitiveness, behind Boot Camp, County Jail, and Day Reporting. Similar results derive from ranking the alternatives with 8 and 12 months imprisonment, except that the law of diminishing returns moves traditional
incarceration even farther down the continuum of severity. In the comparison of alternatives to 8 months imprisonment ("8 Months Index" column),
actual imprisonment ranks as the 8th most punitive sanction out of 10 (excluding Day Fine), with Regular Probation bringing up the rear in terms of
punitiveness. An identical ranking results when comparing the alternatives
to 12 months imprisonment. When looking at the "12 Months Index" col-

umn in Table 3.6, the only alternatives ranked less punitive than prison are Community Service and Regular Probation. In sum, when comparing the alternative sanctions with 4, 8, and 12-months actual imprisonment, traditional incarceration never ranks higher than 4th on the severity scale and slips to 8th when considering longer durations of actual imprisonment.

Table 3.6  Ranking of Sanction Punitiveness Based on Responses from Oklahoma Inmates Who Have Served the Specific Sanction

|  | 4-Month Index | 8-Month Index | 12-Month Index |
|---|---|---|---|
| Most Punitive | Boot Camp | Boot Camp | Boot Camp |
|  | County Jail | County Jail | County Jail |
|  | Day Reporting | Day Reporting | Day Reporting |
|  | Prison | Intermittent Incarceration | Intermittent Incarceration |
|  | Intermittent Incarceration | Halfway House | Halfway House |
|  | Electronic Monitoring | Electronic Monitoring | ISP |
|  | Halfway House | ISP | Electronic Monitoring |
|  | ISP | Prison | Prison |
|  | Community Service | Community Service | Community Service |
| Least Punitive | Probation | Probation | Probation |

a All sanctions in the table are measured by months of time served. The ranking excludes day fines, which are a function of the offender's income, the amount of the fine, and the duration of the sanction (how many days are involved in a fine). Other sanctions are measured according to months served on that sanction.

b We assigned offenders five days per week on intermittent incarceration. This sanction demands that offenders spend weekday nights in county jail, but are free to spend weekend nights at home with family.

c We assigned offenders 20 hours per week, although very few offenders perform that amount of community service per week. If anything, our calculation inflated the punitiveness of community service.

Table 3.7  Average Number of Months of Alternative Sanction Indiana Probationers Are Willing to Serve to Avoid 4, 8, and 12 Months Medium-Security Imprisonment (N = 113)

| Alternative Sanction | Months of Actual Medium Security Imprisonment | | |
|---|---|---|---|
| | 4 Months | 8 Months | 12 Months |
| County Jail | 2.29 | 3.58 | 4.28 |
| Boot Camp | 2.71 | 3.73 | 4.46 |
| Electronic Monitoring | 4.63 | 8.14 | 10.54 |
| Regular Probation | 11.01 | 14.62 | 18.62 |
| Community Service | 9.48 | 12.17 | 14.33 |
| Day Reporting | 7.75 | 10.79 | 14.04 |
| ISP | 4.06 | 7.68 | 13.02 |
| Intermittent Incarceration | 4.97 | 9.40 | 11.98 |
| Halfway House | 5.53 | 7.81 | 12.36 |
| Day Fine | 4.31 | 7.70 | 10.23 |

# Probationers in Indiana

Although the findings from examining exchange rates among probationers in Indiana are discussed in greater detail in Chapter 4 when we discuss racial differences in exchange rates among offenders, the findings from that data are also relevant here. As described in Chapter 2, in 2000 we used a similar instrument as that used with the Oklahoma prisoners to collect data from 113 Indiana probationers to estimate exchange rates among that population. The results presented in Table 3.7 display punishment equivalencies that reflect the average number of months of alternatives that respondents were willing to serve to avoid 4, 8, and 12-months of medium-security imprisonment. The results indicate that, among Indiana probationers, the most punitive sanctions were county jail and boot camp. Of the 10 alternative sanctions presented, only county jail and boot camp were evaluated as more punitive than prison for both the 4 and 8-month indices. To avoid 4 months of imprisonment, these probationers were willing to serve only 2.29 and 2.71 months of county jail and boot camp, respectively, but more than 4 months of all other alternatives. Regarding the least-punitive alternatives, respondents were willing to serve 11.01 months of regular probation, 9.48 months of community service, and 7.75 months of day reporting to avoid 4 months of prison. These results are revisited in greater detail in Chapter 4 when we discuss racial differences in exchange rates.

# Kentucky Parolees and Probationers

As mentioned in Chapter 2, we also collected data from 612 Kentucky probationers and parolees, including 350 Whites and 238 Blacks. All respondents who were not Black or White were excluded from the analyses in this book to allow direct comparisons between Whites and Blacks; thus, the final sample included 588 respondents.

Table 3.8  Descriptive Statistics of the Sample of
Kentucky Probationers and Parolees

|  | N = 588 | Percentage (N/588) |
|---|---|---|
| Gender |  |  |
| Male | 467 | 79.4 |
| Female | 119 | 20.2 |
| Ethnicity |  |  |
| White | 350 | 59.5 |
| Black | 238 | 40.5 |
| Mean Age | 33.29 | n/a |
| Ever Incarcerated in Prison |  |  |
| Yes | 269 | 45.7 |
| No | 300 | 51.0 |
| Ever Served Community Service |  |  |
| Yes | 202 | 34.4 |
| No | 322 | 54.8 |
| Ever Served Halfway House |  |  |
| Yes | 129 | 21.9 |
| No | 430 | 73.1 |
| Ever Served Electronic Monitoring |  |  |
| Yes | 94 | 16.0 |
| No | 417 | 70.9 |
| Currently on Probation or Parole |  |  |
| Probation | 351 | 59.7 |
| Parole | 229 | 38.9 |
| Highest Level Completed Education |  |  |
| 8th grade or less | 50 | 8.5 |
| Some High School | 159 | 27.0 |
| High School Graduate | 228 | 38.8 |
| Some College | 133 | 22.6 |
| College Graduate | 14 | 2.4 |
| Some Graduate/Professional Studies | 3 | .05 |

We collected background information on age, gender, race, education, whether the respondent had ever served time in prison, whether they were presently under probationary or parole supervision, and whether they had previously participated in any of the alternatives examined in the survey. Descriptive statistics for these variables are presented in Table 3.8.

While the entire sample consisted of 588 respondents, each variable under study contained some missing data. As such, percentages in the table do not total 100%. Most respondents were male, and just over one in three was Black. Their average age was 33.29 years. Slightly less than half had spent time in prison, three in five were currently on probation, and just over one in three had previously been sentenced to community service. Smaller proportions had previously served time in a halfway house or on electronic monitoring.

The results contained in Table 3.9 display punishment equivalencies reflecting the average number of months of an alternative that Kentucky probationers and parolees were willing to serve to avoid 12 months of medium security imprisonment. Because respondents were comparing the amount of an alternative sanction they were willing to serve to 12 months incarceration in prison (rather than 4, 8, and 12-months, as in the previous two samples), in effect, these respondents are offering exchange rates that compare the punitiveness of alternative sanctions with prison.

Of the nine alternative sanctions presented, only county jail and boot camp were evaluated as more punitive than prison by the entire sample. To avoid 12 months of imprisonment, respondents were willing to serve an average of only 5.55 and 6.07 months of county jail and boot camp, respectively (exchange rates of approximately one month of jail or boot camp for two months of prison incarcer-

Table 3.9  Exchange Rates among Kentucky Probationers and
Parolees to Avoid 12 Months in State Prison

| Sanction Type | Total Sample (N = 588) |
|---|---|
| County Jail | 5.55 |
| Boot Camp | 6.07 |
| Day Fine | 12.22 |
| Electronic Monitoring | 13.95 |
| Halfway House | 14.42 |
| Intermittent Incarceration | 14.60 |
| Day Reporting | 17.01 |
| Community Service | 22.82 |
| Regular Probation | 23.56 |

ation). They were willing to serve an average of more than 12 months of all other alternatives, although day fine was scored almost the same as prison (12.22 months) by the entire sample (in effect, a 1:1 exchange rate for day fines and prison). Regarding the least punitive alternatives, respondents were willing to serve an average of 23.56 months of regular probation and 22.82 months of community service (this total is derived by dividing 1825.86 hours by 20 hours per week based on four weeks per month) to avoid one year in prison (an exchange rate of approximately 2:1 for both sanctions over prison). Finally, respondents were willing to serve an average of 17.01 months of day reporting to avoid 12 months of prison.

# Attitudinal Predictors of Exchange Rates

Three scales were created to reflect attitudes about alternative sanctions for the Kentucky probationers and parolees. The items used to construct the scales are presented in Appendix B. First, respondents were asked to rate the importance of eight statements (very important, pretty important, somewhat important, and not at all important) as reasons for choosing to *avoid* participation in an alternative sanction. Responses to the statements were coded so that a higher score on the *avoidance scale* reflects greater agreement with reasons to *avoid* alternative sanctions (factor analysis with varimax rotation identified one important factor, Eigenvalue = 3.44). Responses to the eight statements were summed, and Cronbach's alpha for the scale was .806. We expected that those scoring at the high end of the avoidance scale would view alternative sanctions as more punitive when compared to prison than those scoring at the lower end of the scale.

Second, respondents were asked to indicate the importance of five statements (very important, pretty important, somewhat important, and not at all important) as reasons for choosing to *participate* in an alternative sanction. Responses were coded so that a higher score on the *participation scale* reflects greater agreement with reasons to *participate* in alternative sanctions (factor analysis with varimax rotation identified one important factor Eigenvalue = 2.53). Responses to the five statements were summed, and Cronbach's alpha for the scale was .673. We expected that those scoring at the high end of the participation scale would view alternative sanctions as less punitive when compared to prison than those scoring at the lower end of the scale.

Third, respondents were asked to rate the importance (very important, pretty important, somewhat important, and not at all important) of four statements relating to the nature of incarceration in prison as reasons to avoid prison and thus participate in alternatives. Responses to the statements were coded so that a higher score on the *reasons to avoid prison scale* reflects greater agreement that such reasons are important rationales for participation in alternatives (factor analysis with varimax rotation identified one important factor Eigenvalue = 1.65). Responses to the four statements were summed, and the Cronbach's alpha for the scale was .590. We expected those scoring at the high end of the reasons to avoid prison scale will view alternative sanctions as less punitive than those scoring at the lower end of the scale.

We then used OLS regression to examine the impact of the predictor variables outlined above on the amount (in hours) of community service and the amount (in months) of electronic monitoring and halfway house probationers and parolees would serve to avoid 12 months imprisonment.

The results presented in Table 3.10 reflect the results of regressing the number of months of halfway house and electronic monitoring and the number of hours of community service that respondents would serve to avoid 12 months imprisonment on a number of demographic, contextual, and attitudinal variables in the Kentucky probationer and parolee sample. Previous incarceration in

**Table 3.10  Multivariate OLS Regression Amount of 3 Community Sanctions Offenders Will Serve to Avoid 12 Months Imprisonment***

| Predictor | Community Service (N=517) | | Electronic Monitoring (N=517) | | Halfway House (N=516) | |
|---|---|---|---|---|---|---|
| | Beta | Sig | Beta | Sig | Beta | Sig |
| Have Served Time in Prison | .042 | .176 | -.119 | .004 | -.101 | .015 |
| Black | -.170 | .000 | -.136 | .001 | -.085 | .029 |
| Age | -.174 | .000 | -.165 | .000 | -.096 | .018 |
| Male | -.031 | .231 | -.093 | .025 | -.085 | .025 |
| Reasons to Avoid Alternative Scale | -.155 | .000 | -.181 | .000 | -.055 | .113 |
| Reasons to Participate in Alternative Scale | .003 | .478 | .071 | .066 | .037 | .225 |
| Reasons to Avoid Prison Scale | .090 | .034 | -.031 | .262 | -.026 | .301 |
| $R^2$/Adjusted $R^2$ | .088 | .075 | .137 | .126 | .052 | .039 |

* Community Service is measured in hours while Electronic Monitoring and Halfway House are measured in months. All models are estimated using one-tailed test of statistical significance.

prison, race, age, gender, and the scale representing reasons to avoid an alternative sanction all significantly impacted the amount of one or more alternatives that offenders are willing to serve. Those who had served time in prison and males would endure fewer months of electronic monitoring and halfway house to avoid 12 months in a medium security prison. Further, Whites, younger respondents, and those who scored lower on the avoidance scale agreed to serve longer durations of *all three sanctions* than their counterparts to avoid 12 months in prison.

Regarding the other attitudinal indexes, respondents who scored higher on the reasons to participate in an alternative sanction were no more likely to be willing to serve any of the sanctions than offenders with lower scores on the scale. Finally, those who scored higher on the reasons to avoid prison index would serve more months of community service, but not electronic monitoring or halfway house placement. Neither of the three regression models presented in Table 3.10 accounted for much variation in punishment equivalency ratings. The models comparing community service and electronic monitoring to prison accounted for 8.8% and 13.7% of the total variance in these ratings, respectively, while the one comparing halfway house placement with prison accounted for only 5.2%.

Finally, we constructed a ranking that compares the responses of the three samples regarding the perceived punitiveness of community service, electronic monitoring, halfway house, and five other sanctions to 12 months of imprisonment. In doing so, we follow the calculation of sentence duration described earlier in this chapter for the Oklahoma prisoners, particularly for sanctions measured in hours. We again divided the total number of hours an inmate would serve by 80 to arrive at the number of months of community service the inmate would serve to avoid a specified length of imprisonment. We thus are able to compare the relative severity ranking of all three samples of offenders under study here.

The results presented in Table 3.11 indicate that prison is not viewed by any group as the most severe sanction. For the entire sample, both boot camp and county jail are rated as more onerous than prison. Additionally, all three groups agreed that regular probation was the least punitive sanction and community service was the second least punitive. The ranking of the other alternative sanctions varied somewhat depending on the sample under study.

# Discussion

Consistent with previous work, we determine that while some offenders may perceive imprisonment as the most punitive correctional sanction, this

Table 3.11  Severity Rankings of Correctional Sanctions Based on a
12 Month Index for Oklahoma Prisoners, Indiana Probationers,
and Kentucky Probationers and Parolees

| Severity Ranking | Oklahoma Prisoners | Indiana Probationers | Kentucky Probationers and Parolees |
|---|---|---|---|
| Most Severe | Boot Camp | County Jail | County Jail |
| | County Jail | Boot Camp | Boot Camp |
| | Day reporting | Electronic Monitoring | Prison |
| | Intermittent Incarceration | Intermittent Incarceration | Electronic Monitoring |
| | Halfway House | Prison | Halfway House |
| | ISP | Halfway House | Intermittent Incarceration |
| | Electronic Monitoring | ISP | * |
| | Prison | Day Reporting | Day reporting |
| | Community Service | Community Service | Community Service |
| Least Severe | Regular Probation | Regular Probation | Regular Probation |

* Day Fine is not ranked in this scale, as day fines are a function of the offender's income, the amount of the fine, and how many days are involved in the fine. With the exception of community service, all other fines are measured according to the number of months served on that sanction to avoid prison. We calculated a month as the number of hours of community service the respondent told us they would serve to avoid 12 months in prison divided by 80 (we felt 20 hours represented the "average" number of hours per week for community service times 4 weeks per month).

is not true for all or even most of them. Based on our study of Oklahoma inmates, Indiana probationers, and Kentucky probationers and parolees, we suggest that offender-generated exchange rates are primarily influenced by offenders' demographic characteristics (specifically age, race, and to some degree gender), prior prison experience, perceptions of the inconvenience, intrusiveness, and overall punitiveness of intermediate sanctions, and by conditions that may affect the pain and suffering associated with imprisonment.

In our sample, age has a consistent, significant impact on penal exchange rates even when controlling for other potentially important factors. For each of the three intermediate sanctions examined in detail here, age registers a negative association with the duration of the sanction offenders would serve to avoid imprisonment. Our findings suggest that older offenders are more likely to reject alternatives and choose prison instead, and older offenders will not serve as much of an alternative as will younger ones. We suspect that older offenders may view alternative sanctions as more of a gamble than younger ones. They may think the chances of revocation are too high, and if they fail to complete the sanction, they will be revoked back to prison to serve out their original sentence—thereby extending their time under correctional supervision. It is also likely that older offenders may have had more experience serving time in prison, and the combination of prior prison experience with age serves to impact penal exchange rates in a significant way (see below). The results presented here also suggest that gender, race, and prior prison experience influence choice of exchange rates as well. These findings are discussed in detail in later chapters and will not be addressed here.

Perceptions of the inconvenience, intrusiveness, and punitiveness of intermediate sanctions seem to be strongly influenced by: a) the conduct and personalities of programmatic staff and parole/probation officers; b) high failure and revocation rates associated with many alternative sanctions; and c) how offenders subjectively rate the overall severity of prison compared to alternative sanctions. These issues are addressed in our attitudinal measures, one of which (reasons to avoid alternative sanctions) generates a significant impact on all three exchange rates examined in Table 3.10. The higher that offenders scored on this scale, the less of each alternative they were willing to serve to avoid imprisonment. Along with age and race, this measure produced the strongest and most consistent impact on the offender's willingness to participate in the alternative sanctions presented in Table 3.10. And though conditions related to the pain and suffering of imprisonment had a significant impact on only one exchange rate (community service compared to prison), offenders with experience in several institutions observed that conditions in some are harder on inmates than others, and that prisons vary considerably in the amount of pain and suffering they may inflict.

# Factors That Influence Variation in Exchange Rates among Offenders

Given that the exchange rates findings presented above may be somewhat counterintuitive (and contradictory to the present body of knowledge regarding deterrence and sentencing), in this section we explain why offenders might prefer prison over alternatives, and why many rate alternatives as more punitive than imprisonment.

As our findings demonstrated here, a number of offenders with prior prison experience (or who were currently on parole) chose to serve longer amounts of prison than alternative sanctions served in the community. These findings undermine classical deterrence doctrine that would claim that those who are imprisoned for a crime would be less likely to re-offend and less likely to prefer prison over a community based sanction. Contrary to classical deterrence theory, offenders in prison or with prison experience were more likely to choose to do the time and be released, rather than "gamble" by investing time and effort in completing an alternative sanction with a high perceived likelihood of revocation, unacceptable restrictions, and supervision by hostile probation and parole officers.

The exchange rate evidence for offenders suggests that reasons for avoiding or participating in alternative sanctions have little to do with the specifics of the program or the institution in which inmates are serving time (i.e., program rules too strict, prison too harsh on inmates), but have more to do with the manner in which these programs are administered. Consequently, the most important impacts on whether a person would choose to serve an alternative sanction in the community may have more to do with the people operating the program than the actual program itself. If this is the case, then these findings would strengthen the conclusions of deterrence and rational choice scholars regarding the "indirect" sanctions or costs and the greater deterrent effect they have on recidivism (Grasmick and Bursik, 1990; and Williams & Hawkins, 1986).

Qualitative research provides further evidence to support these findings. This research suggests that offenders who have acquired knowledge and experience about living in prison appear less fearful of prison than those without such experience. Williams et al. (2008) suggest that once an inmate has served time in prison, prison is less of an unknown, and thus less likely to be feared. In much the same way that military boot camp is a daunting experience until a soldier has survived it, prison is an environment that many may dread until they have actually experienced it. After that initial incarceration experience, at least to some, prison may then be seen as easier than an alternative sanction—particularly if they perceive their sentence as unjust, unfair, or excessive, and are defiant toward that sentence as suggested above or they feel the community sanction has a high likelihood of revocation. Among inmates with experience serving time, imprisonment becomes familiar; contrasted against an unfamiliar, unpredictable community sanction, these experienced offenders prefer the stability and predictability of the prison sentence to the alternative (whatever that may be). Persons without that same prior experience in prison may be more fearful of it, and will opt to do the alternative—and a longer duration of it—in order to avoid prison. As such, this finding calls into question the deterrent value of imprisonment, particularly because those who have served prison are more likely to choose prison over alternative sanctions compared to those with no prison experience (May et al., 2005).

While this argument may seem strange to those not familiar with serving time, this perspective may also explain our findings that many offenders would rather serve a longer prison term than a short jail sentence. Fleisher (1995, p. 164) supported this argument when he described an offender who preferred three or four years at the State Penitentiary before doing one year in the county jail, because "It be too hard to have a good time up in that ol' jail. Now, in prison, that's different." Our own interviews of probationers and parolees further support this choice by seasoned offenders, as evidenced by the following responses providing explanations for why an offender would choose jail over prison:

> … cause in prison, you know, you can probably go outside, you can play basketball, lift weights, smoke cigarettes, whatever. In jail you can't do none of that. (Respondent #2)
> Because prison time's easier when you've got a gym to go to, basketball, softball, horseshoes, the library, and if you ain't there, you're in your cell, you got color TV. (Respondent #81)

Fleisher goes on to note, "Prison isn't a risk that worries street hustlers. Things such as limited freedom, loss of privacy, violence, and variant sexual activity, which might frighten lawful citizens, don't frighten them" (1995, p. 164). In fact, Santos (2003, p. 216) suggests that after five years or so, life in prison "… becomes normal and predictable, although within a restricted, harsh, and sometimes inhumane closed society" (2003, p. 216). In speaking of a fellow inmate, "Ron," Santos notes the following:

> Ronald knew that his initial prison term would enhance his status, that it would show he could take the punishment and survive a stint

in even the toughest of conditions. He would emerge from prison with more power and street credibility than he had when he went it, enabling him to expand his criminal enterprise.... Influenced by twenty years of living in a urban ghetto, with family members, acquaintances, and role models all having served time, Ronald was committed to a life of crime and what he considered easy money. For Ronald, a stretch in confinement was an obligation incidental to the choices he made. As a young black thug who quit school in the ninth grade, being locked up was something he knew he would face more than once in his life" (Santos, 2006:15–16).

Our own qualitative work supports these arguments. Over one in eight probationers and parolees we interviewed said that prison is easier than the alternative or that the alternatives were harder than prison. One in six responded that an offender can get out of prison quicker than if they served the alternative. Furthermore, one in ten said that the reason offenders would choose to serve prison time over an alternative was because they were afraid of getting into trouble and having the alternative revoked. Probationers and parolees also suggested that offenders would choose prison over an alternative because they "don't want to face their responsibilities," "they use prison to escape the rules of the alternative sanction," or "they do not want to deal with the probation officers" (Williams et al., 2008). Their comments, included below, provide further context for that choice:

I'd rather go to prison than do the probation. It's hard, they come to your house, they belittle you, they degrade you, no matter how good you do, no matter how well you turn your life around. (Respondent #5)

Well, usually the alternatives are a lot longer and more strict, and you usually end up violating and you end up going back to prison anyway, so it's, in the long run, it's just easier to do your prison time because they make it so difficult. It strings it out longer when you don't do the prison time. (Respondent #14)

I think, because, prison time usually you can get your time out of the way and be done with it, but say you're on some kind of alternative, and that last month, you mess up, they might wipe that whole time out and give you a whole other sentence. (Respondent #26)

Qualitative work also indicates that among those with a history of imprisonment, intermediate sanctions may carry a sort of stigma. Based on the authors' interviews with offenders in a variety of settings, experienced cons often frown on offenders who volunteer for the intrusive supervision and restrictions of intermediate sanctions. For many older and more experienced offenders, then, willingness to serve an intermediate sanction may be seen as a "copout" of sorts, carrying a stigma of being reserved for younger and weaker inmates, and is to be avoided by those who have adapted to living in prison.

The pain of imprisonment can also be related to characteristics of the offender or the crime committed. It is true that those convicted of certain offenses (child molesters and rapists, for example) are often abused by other inmates, and first-timers generally have a tougher time than experienced cons. As noted by Morris and Tonry, what looks like an equal sentence of 12 months imprisonment, "… may, in practice, vary substantially in its impact on the offender" (1990, p. 102). One might expect, therefore, that the prison environment itself would generate an important contextual influence on penal exchange rates.

Given the findings presented here, we feel that important questions about why certain groups (e.g., Blacks, males, and ex-prisoners) rate prison as less punitive than their White, female, and non-institutionalized counterparts warrant further exploration. As such, we explore those findings in the following chapters.

CHAPTER 4

# RACE AND GENDER DIFFERENCES IN EXCHANGE RATES

In the previous chapter, we revealed convincing evidence that the continuum of sanctions proposed by Morris and Tonry almost two decades ago (with probation on one end and prison on the other) may not be as tenable as it first appeared. Increasingly it seems that offenders who receive identical punishments may "perceive the severity of their punishment to be very different due to differences in their age, race, sex, prior punishment history, or other factors" (Spelman, 1995, p. 132). For example, Apospori and Alpert (1993) found that experience with legal sanctions raised individuals' perceptions of the severity of those sanctions. Petersilia and Deschenes (1994a, 1994b) noted that inmates who were married and/or had children ranked incarceration as more severe than those who were single, while inmates who were single ranked financial penalties (e.g., fines, restitution) as more severe than inmates who were married. And although Petersilia and Deschenes found no significant differences in rankings of sanction severity by race, prior prison experience, employment history, drug dependence, or how safe the inmate felt in prison, their limited sample (48 male inmates) may have precluded the discovery of such differences. Spelman (1995) observed that an offender's age, number of prior incarcerations, and type of offense for which they were incarcerated was all associated with a greater preference for a jail term than for an alternative sanction. Older offenders preferred brief imprisonment rather than intermediate sanctions of longer lengths, and those who had served time in prison were more likely to choose another jail term over a relatively longer ISP term than were those with no prior prison experience. Drug users and dealers were less likely to prefer a jail term over intermediate sanctions compared to offenders arrested for violent and property crimes (Spelman, 1995). Crouch (1993) also reported a preference for prison over probation among offenders who were older, unmarried, widely exposed to crime and institutional corrections, and among those who believed that probation had grown stricter.

In this chapter, we continue that discussion of differential experiences of correctional sanctions by examining differences in exchange rates by race and gender. We first use data from 151 Indiana probationers to examine perceptions of the severity of 10 alternative sanctions compared to 4, 8, and 12-months of imprisonment. The data reveal stark racial differences as 1) Blacks rate every alternative sanction as more punitive than do Whites, 2) a higher percent of Blacks refuse to participate in each alternative sanction, and 3) Blacks identify more strongly with reasons to avoid alternatives. These factors contribute to significant race differences in how offenders rank the punitiveness of criminal sanctions. We then use data from Oklahoma prisoners and Kentucky probationers and parolees to examine gender differences in exchange rates. These data reveal that males, across all samples and for practically all alternatives, rate alternative sanctions as more punitive than females

# Race and Attitudes toward Criminal Justice and Punishment

It is not surprising that Blacks perceive an unequal distribution of justice by race in the United States. While Blacks represent only 13% of the total U.S. population, they account for 42% of prisoners and black males were six times more likely than white males to be incarcerated in 2007 (West & Sabol, 2008). A black male born today has a 28% chance of serving time in a state or federal prison at some point in his life (Mauer, 1999). Sadly, with so many young black men under criminal justice supervision, involvement in the justice system is viewed by many Blacks—particularly those in low-income and high-crime communities—as an expected rite of passage (Irwin & Austin, 1997).

As might be expected, public attitudes toward criminal justice and punishment vary by respondents' demographic characteristics. With perhaps one obvious exception (Frank, Brandl, Cullen, & Stichman, 1996), research has consistently found that Blacks have more negative views toward the criminal justice system than do Whites (Albrecht & Green, 1977; Brandl, Frank, Worden, & Bynum, 1994; Cao, Frank, & Cullen, 1996; Flanagan & Longmire, 1996; Hagan & Albonetti, 1982; Henderson, Cullen, Cao, Browning, & Kopache, 1997; Roberts & Stalans, 2000) and this racial divide characterizes public opinion about American criminal justice today.

National opinion polls have revealed that Blacks are significantly more likely than Whites to agree that Blacks are treated more harshly by the country's criminal justice system, that police protection in black neighborhoods is worse than in white neighborhoods, and that racism against Blacks among law enforcement officers is widespread. In addition, Blacks are more likely than Whites to report little or no confidence that law enforcement agencies treat Blacks and

Whites equally in their community and to admit that they have been treated unfairly by police officers because of their race (Pastore & Maguire, 2008; Tuch & Weitzer, 1997; Weitzer & Tuch, 1999).

Observed racial differences in perceptions of "criminal injustice" (a composite measure of items reflecting problems associated with the police, courts, juries, judges, and/or lawyers) are reported to vary by socioeconomic status as well. And although there is some disagreement regarding whether the greatest racial differences are between Whites and affluent Blacks (Hagan & Albonetti, 1982) or between Whites and low-income Blacks (Henderson et al., 1997), research continues to find that "African-Americans see the criminal justice system as racially biased, while the majority of Whites generally believe the system is racially neutral and reflects the ideal of equal treatment before the law" (Henderson et al., 1997, p. 455). Surveys and polls consistently show that a larger proportion of Blacks than Whites have less favorable opinions about various components of justice, including police, courts, judges, juries, and lawyers (Cao et al., 1996; Roberts & Stalans, 2000; Tuch & Weitzer,1997). According to the most recent available data, a greater proportion of Blacks than Whites have "very little" confidence in both the criminal justice system and the police, are more likely to feel that the police treat "one or more groups unfairly," are more fearful that they will be stopped and arrested by the police when they are innocent, are more likely to perceive that there is police brutality in their communities, feel that courts deal "too harshly" with criminals , and register "low" ratings of the honesty and ethical standards of police and judges (Pastore & Maguire, 2008).

Given that these perceptions of police, judges, and courts characterize Blacks' views of the justice system, it would not be surprising to find that many black offenders view alternative sanctions with suspicion, particularly if they expect poor treatment or discrimination by program officers and consider the risk of revocation to be high. If Henderson et al. (1997) are correct, suspicion regarding the community-sanctions component of criminal justice may be even more pronounced among low-income Blacks, particularly those who have experienced arrest, conviction, and/or punishment.

The voluminous literature on public attitudes toward punishment has generally found smaller racial differences (Flanagan & Longmire, 1996; Jacoby & Cullen, 1999; Miller, Rossi, & Simpson, 1986; Warr, Meier, & Erickson, 1983). Research has revealed a surprising degree of consensus across demographic groups regarding the kinds of punishments that are appropriate for different offenses, although people do not necessarily agree on the amount of a sanction that should be applied to a specific offense. Miller et al. (1986, p. 331) reported that, in response to vignettes describing an offense, an offender, and a proposed punishment, Blacks were "more strongly influenced by the duration of the prison term when forming harshness judgments ...." regardless of the offense, and were "slightly more influenced by the social characteristics of the offenders." Nevertheless, Blacks and Whites generally agreed on the type of punishment. Black women, however, appeared to make harsher judgments than other demographic groups, perhaps because of their greater "proximity to crime" and concerns about being victimized. These factors were found to be positively related to a preference for harsher punishments, although Jacoby and Cullen (1999) found that variation in the "punishment threshold" did not differ significantly by race.

Although Blacks have historically registered greater opposition than Whites to the death penalty as a punishment for murder (Bohm, 1991; Durham, Ford, & Kinkade, 1996; Pastore & Maguire, 2008), Blacks and Whites have evidenced greater agreement about the appropriate punishment for crimes than they have about attitudes toward various components of the justice system (Flanagan & Longmire, 1996; Jacoby & Cullen, 1999; Miller et al., 1986; Roberts & Stalans, 2000; Rossi, Simpson, & Miller, 1985; Warr et al., 1983).

# Race Differences in Exchange Rates

Until 1995, only three published studies explored racial differences in perceptions of sanction severity. As we noted earlier, Petersilia and Deschenes (1994a, 1994b) failed to find a significant racial difference (but used only 48 male inmates in their efforts). Crouch (1993, p. 67) observed that "being African-American is the strongest predictor of a preference for prison," and Spelman (1995, p. 122) found that "the most important predictor of preference for a jail term is the offender's race."

In this section, we focus primarily on racial differences in the perceived severity of sanctions. As noted previously, extant research suggests that offender characteristics may significantly influence perceptions and rankings of the severity of punishments. In the current chapter, we examine racial differences in 1) preferences for prison, rather than alternatives; 2) the duration of alternatives that offenders are willing to serve to avoid imprisonment; and 3) reasons for avoiding alternative sanctions. Based on offender surveys, we also generate a ranking of sanction severity by race that includes traditional imprisonment, county jail, regular probation, and eight other alternative sanctions.

We used data collected from 136 Indiana probationers described in previous chapters to examine racial differences in exchange rates. Work cited earlier suggested that race is one of several factors that are likely to influence

offenders' perceptions of the severity of sanctions. In Table 4.1, we demonstrated that, among the Indiana probationers, white and black respondents
were similar in most ways. As such, alternative explanations for the observed
relationship between race and views on the severity of sanctions (presented in
Tables 4.4–4.7) are unlikely, given the nonsignificant differences between black
and white probationers on multiple sociodemographic and corrections-related
factors. The results presented in Table 4.1 reveal basic socio-demographic information about our 136 black and white respondents. Observe that the two
groups were similar with respect to age (Blacks averaging 30.45 years and Whites
32.16 years), gender distribution (71.9% of black respondents were male compared to 82.3% of Whites), education (very similar with regard to levels of education achieved and average education level), having children (80.7% of black
respondents and 70.5% of white respondents have children), having had children live with them (33.3% of black respondents versus 40% of Whites), having served time in county jail (74% of Blacks compared to 80% of Whites),
and having a previous felony conviction (91.2% of Blacks compared to 96.2%
of Whites). In general, our black and white probationers resembled one another
in most ways except for rural/urban location (only one black respondent was
generated by the rural probation office), and percent who were serving their
present sentence for a drug conviction (36.8% of Blacks compared to 16.7% of
Whites). Thus, though we do not present multivariate results (which would be
highly suspect due to the small sample size), we argue that any racial differences
in punishment equivalencies and severity rankings noted here were likely not
due to the minimal racial differences in offender characteristics presented in Table
4.1.

In Table 4.2, we present punishment equivalencies that reflect the average number of months of alternatives that respondents (black and white together) were willing to serve to avoid 4, 8, and 12-months of medium-security
imprisonment, and indicated that the most punitive sanctions were county
jail and boot camp. Of the 10 alternative sanctions presented, only county
jail and boot camp were evaluated as more punitive than prison for both the
4 and 8-month indices. To avoid 4 months of imprisonment, these probationers were willing to serve only 2.29 and 2.71 months of county jail and boot
camp, respectively, but more than 4 months of all other alternatives. Regarding the least punitive alternatives, respondents were willing to serve 11.01
months of regular probation, 9.48 months of community service, and 7.75
months of day reporting to avoid 4 months of prison. Although the number
of months that respondents were willing to serve in alternatives increased, the
8-months index demonstrated a similar pattern. County jail (3.56 months)
and boot camp (3.73 months) were again viewed as more punitive than

### Table 4.1 Descriptive Statistics of Black and White Respondents

| | Blacks and Whites (N=136) | Blacks Only (N=57) | Whites Only (N=79) |
|---|---|---|---|
| Age | 31.5 | 30.45 | 32.16 |
| Gender | | | |
| Male | 106 (77.9%) | 41 (71.9%) | 65 (82.3%) |
| Female | 30 (22.1%) | 16 (28.1%) | 14 (17.7%) |
| Education | | | |
| 8th grade or less | 3 (2.2%) | 0 (0.0%) | 3 (3.8%) |
| Some high school | 37 (27.4%) | 16 (28.1%) | 21 (26.9%) |
| H.S. degree | 49 (36.3%) | 20 (35.1%) | 29 (37.2%) |
| Some college | 25 (18.5%) | 15 (26.3%) | 10 (12.8%) |
| College degree | 11 (8.1%) | 2 (3.5%) | 9 (11.5%) |
| Grad/Prof school | 1 (0.7%) | 1 (1.8%) | 0 (0.0%) |
| Other (Trade) | 9 (6.7%) | 3 (5.3%) | 6 (7.7%) |
| Average education (8th grade or less = 1 Grad/Prof = 6) | 3.06 | 3.11 | 3.01 |
| Have Children? | | | |
| Yes | 101 (74.8%) | 46 (80.7%) | 55 (70.5%) |
| No | 34 (25.2%) | 11 (19.3%) | 23 (29.5%) |
| Children Lived with Respondent? | | | |
| Yes | 37 (37.0%) | 15 (33.3%) | 22 (40.0%) |
| No | 63 (63.0%) | 30 (66.6%) | 33 (60.0%) |
| Ever Served Time in County Jail? | | | |
| Yes | 97 (77.6%) | 37 (74.0%) | 60 (80.0%) |
| No | 28 (22.4%) | 13 (26.0%) | 15 (20.0%) |
| Probation Office | | | |
| Rural | 23 (16.9%) | 1 (1.8%) | 22 (27.8%) |
| Urban | 113 (83.1%) | 56 (98.2%) | 57 (72.2%) |
| Ever Had a Felony Conviction? | | | |
| Yes | 127 (94.1%) | 52 (91.2%) | 75 (96.2%) |
| No | 8 (5.9%) | 5 (8.8%) | 3 (3.8%) |
| Present Sentence for Drugs? | | | |
| Yes | 34 (25.3%) | 21 (36.8%) | 13 (16.7%) |
| No | 101 (74.8%) | 36 (63.2%) | 65 (83.3%) |

Table 4.2  Average Number of Months of Alternative Sanction
Probationers Are Willing to Serve to Avoid 4, 8, and 12 Months
Medium Security Imprisonment

| Alternative Sanction | Months of Actual Medium-Security Imprisonment | | |
|---|---|---|---|
| | 4 Months | 8 Months | 12 Months |
| County Jail | 2.29 | 3.58 | 4.28 |
| Boot Camp | 2.71 | 3.73 | 4.46 |
| Electronic Monitoring | 4.63 | 8.14 | 10.54 |
| Regular Probation | 11.01 | 14.62 | 18.62 |
| Community Service | 9.48 | 12.17 | 14.33 |
| Day Reporting | 7.75 | 10.79 | 14.04 |
| ISP | 4.06 | 7.68 | 13.02 |
| Intermittent Incarceration | 4.97 | 9.40 | 11.98 |
| Halfway House | 5.53 | 7.81 | 12.36 |
| Day Fine | 4.31 | 7.70 | 10.23 |

prison, while regular probation (14.62 months), community service (12.17 months), and day reporting (10.79 months) were once again rated as the least punitive alternatives. The same pattern was seen, with minor exceptions, for the 12-months index. Once again, county jail (4.28 months) and boot camp (4.46 months) were viewed as significantly more punitive than prison, while electronic monitoring (EM) (10.54) and day fine (10.23) were rated as slightly more punitive than imprisonment. Furthermore, as with the 4 and 8-months indices, regular probation, community service, and day reporting were rated as the least punitive.

We also found that the additional amount of time that these probationers were willing to serve on an alternative sanction did not increase proportionately as the duration of prison increased from 4 to 8 to 12-months. The respondents were not willing to serve three times as much of a given alternative to avoid 12 months of imprisonment as they would to avoid 4 months of imprisonment. Although the duration of imprisonment was multiplied by three, they were willing to risk serving three times as much of the alternative only in the case of ISP (4.06 months on the 4-months index and 13.02 months on the 12-months index). With regard to the 12-months index, the amount of the alternative-county jail, boot camp, regular probation, community service, and day reporting—that the respondents would serve usually did not exceed twice the amount they would serve to avoid just 4 months of imprisonment. As will be demonstrated, the law of diminishing returns has significant implications for how Blacks and Whites rank the severity of criminal sanctions.

# Racial Differences in Perceptions of Alternatives Compared to Prison

As mentioned earlier, two previous studies have suggested that Blacks tend to view prison as less punitive than do Whites and may view alternatives as more severe than do Whites (Crouch, 1993; Spelman, 1995). Crouch suggested that Blacks may adjust to prison more easily than may other groups, perhaps because a large proportion of inner-city black men are imprisoned and routinely find friends and relatives already in prison who can provide them with information, material goods, and protection. Crouch noted that the urban underclass lifestyle makes the potential violence and deprivation of a prison term seem less threatening to Blacks than to Whites:

> Because the ghettos from which many African-Americans come are often unpredictable and threatening environments, they learn to emphasize self-protection and to develop physical and psychological toughness. This toughness protects African-American prisoners and enables them to dominate others behind bars, especially Whites.... it suggests that race and ethnicity may influence how offenders view the relative costs of punitiveness of criminal sanctions (Crouch, 1993, p. 71).

For these reasons, Crouch believes that given a choice between prison and a range of alternative sanctions, African-Americans would choose prison more often than would Whites. Blacks are more likely than Whites to be sent to prison, are likely more familiar with what to expect in prison, and are more likely to find "homies" there, circumstances that may make prison less threatening.

There are other reasons to expect that Blacks would be more likely than Whites to choose prison over a range of alternative sanctions. Blacks (more than Whites) may tend to feel that they will be subject to abuse or harassment under alternative sanctions and thus may feel that they are more likely to be revoked back to prison. This implies that Blacks and Whites entertain different "risk assessments" when it comes to evaluating whether participation in an alternative is a gamble they are willing to take. Rather than view prison as less punitive than alternatives, it is therefore possible that prison contains less uncertainty, and many offenders (black and white) may wish to serve out their terms and be released with no strings attached, rather than invest time and effort in an alternative sanction involving potentially abusive program officers and a high likelihood of program violation and revocation. However, questions remain about whether such risk assessments vary by race and, if so, why.

To address these questions, we began by examining the percentage of white and black respondents who refused to participate in alternative sanctions to avoid 4, 8, and 12-months of imprisonment. The numbers in Table 4.3 represent the percentage of probationers who would choose prison rather than any duration of an alternative sanction. Within each imprisonment index (4, 8, and 12-months) and for every alternative in Table 4.3, Blacks were more likely to choose prison than Whites. The modal pattern is that 20–30% of Blacks will chose prison rather than the alternative compared to 1–10% of Whites. Given the choice between prison and county jail, boot camp, EM, and halfway house, Blacks were two to three times more likely to choose prison than Whites. With regard to regular probation, day reporting, ISP, intermittent incarceration, and day fine, Blacks were anywhere from three to six times more likely to choose prison than Whites. For example, in the four month index, 24.6% of Blacks choose prison over ISP, compared to only 4% of Whites. Clearly, when given a choice between prison and alternative sanctions, African-Americans voiced a stronger preference for prison than Whites.

Of additional interest are race differences in the amount of the alternative offenders are willing to serve. The results presented in Table 4.4 offer race comparisons in the average number of months of an alternative sanction that probationers are willing to serve to avoid 4, 8, and 12 months' imprisonment. For each alternative and within each length of imprisonment, Blacks rated the alternative sanction as more punitive than did Whites. For example, whereas Whites were willing to serve 6.32 months of EM to avoid 4 months of imprisonment, Blacks were willing to serve only 2.96 months. In many instances, Whites were willing to serve twice as much of the alternative as Blacks to avoid a specific duration of imprisonment. Furthermore, the racial differences presented in Table 4.4 were significant at the .01 level for all comparisons except county jail. Not only were Blacks more likely to choose prison than were Whites (see Table 4.3), but Whites were willing to serve significantly more of each alternative than were Blacks.

Table 4.3  Percentages of Probationers Who Refuse to Participate
in the Specified Alternative Sanction to Avoid 4, 8, or 12 Months
of Medium-Security Imprisonment

| Alternative Sanction | Months of Actual Imprisonment | | | | | |
|---|---|---|---|---|---|---|
| | 4 Months | | 8 Months | | 12 Months | |
| | Black | White | Black | White | Black | White |
| County Jail | 23.6 | 17.0 | 24.1 | 13.5 | 25.0 | 15.4 |
| Boot Camp | 25.5 | 18.9 | 21.8 | 15.4 | 24.5 | 15.7 |
| Electronic Monitoring | 22.2 | 13.2 | 20.4 | 11.3 | 17.0 | 11.5 |
| Regular Probation | 8.9 | 3.6 | 5.4 | 1.8 | 8.9 | 1.8 |
| Community Service | 16.1 | 9.6 | 14.3 | 7.5 | 17.9 | 7.7 |
| Day Reporting | 25.5 | 1.9 | 23.6 | 1.9 | 24.1 | 1.9 |
| ISP | 25.0 | 3.8 | 25.0 | 3.8 | 26.8 | 3.8 |
| Intermittent Incarceration | 23.2 | 13.2 | 25.0 | 9.4 | 25.0 | 9.6 |
| Halfway House | 18.5 | 7.4 | 18.5 | 7.4 | 19.2 | 7.5 |
| Day Fine | 36.4 | 13.5 | 34.5 | 13.2 | 34.5 | 15.4 |

Table 4.4  Average Months of Alternative Sanction Probationers are
Willing to Serve to Avoid 4, 8, and 12 Months Medium-Security
Imprisonment. Comparison of Blacks v. Whites*

| Alternative Sanction | Months of Actual Medium-Security Imprisonment | | | | | |
|---|---|---|---|---|---|---|
| | 4 Months | | 8 Months | | 12 Months | |
| | Black | White | Black | White | Black | White |
| County Jail | 2.07 | 2.51 | 3.28 | 3.88 | 3.63 | 4.92 |
| Boot Camp | 1.98 | 3.47 | 3.05 | 4.44 | 3.58 | 5.37 |
| Electronic Monitoring | 2.96 | 6.32 | 5.72 | 10.60 | 7.13 | 14.02 |
| Regular Probation | 7.43 | 14.65 | 11.04 | 18.27 | 15.12 | 22.18 |
| Community Service | 5.73 | 13.52 | 8.36 | 16.19 | 10.68 | 18.27 |
| Day Reporting | 4.45 | 11.23 | 7.49 | 14.29 | 10.00 | 18.23 |
| ISP | 2.96 | 5.23 | 5.80 | 9.66 | 8.96 | 17.30 |
| Intermittent Incarceration | 3.50 | 6.53 | 6.79 | 12.04 | 9.43 | 14.73 |
| Halfway House | 4.13 | 6.93 | 6.06 | 9.56 | 9.23 | 15.43 |
| Day Fine | 2.87 | 5.83 | 5.27 | 10.23 | 7.67 | 12.94 |

* Mean racial differences by sanction within each duration index are significant at $p < .01$
for all race comparisons with the exception of those for county jail

# What May Account for the
# Observed Racial Differences?

As can be seen in Table 4.1, roughly twice as many Blacks as Whites reported a drug offense (35.7% versus 16.1%) and experience with EM (45.8% versus 27.3%). It is possible that drug offenders and those who have prior experience with EM may find alternatives less desirable than a sentence of incarceration and may be willing to serve a lesser duration of alternatives because of concerns about the close supervision and drug testing associated with alternative sanctions. Previous work (Apospori & Alpert, 1993; Wood & Grasmick, 1999) has suggested that prior experience serving alternatives may influence one's rating of the severity of alternatives and one's willingness to participate in them. In other words, the observed racial differences noted in Tables 4.2–4.4 may be attributable to racial differences in having a drug conviction or prior experience with EM. To explore this possibility, we looked for racial differences in the amount of alternatives the respondents were willing to serve and their preference for prison over alternatives while controlling for prior drug convictions and prior experience with EM.

First, we compared all drug offenders (n = 29) with all nondrug offenders (n = 83) in the sample (one respondent did not provide a response to the question assessing whether they were a drug offender). The results were consistent with the idea that drug offenders were unwilling to serve as much of each alternative as were nondrug offenders and more often chose prison over any duration of an alternative for each alternative. Thus, the association between drug offending and alternatives operated in the suspected direction, although none of the comparisons was statistically significant. Nevertheless, the results suggest that drug offenders may perceive a greater risk in serving alternatives that require random drug testing, as was detailed in the description of most alternative sanctions in the survey.

We then looked for racial differences among the drug offenders in the amount of alternatives they were willing to serve and in their preference for prison. Among the drug offenders, Whites (n = 9) were willing to serve more of an alternative than were Blacks (n = 20) in 25 of 30 comparisons (10 alternatives multiplied by the three duration indices), with 11 of the comparisons achieving significance (p < .05). The racial differences observed in the main sample were essentially replicated when we controlled for drug convictions, although because of the small number of cases, findings of statistical significance were harder to achieve. In just over two thirds (21 of 30) of the racial comparisons, black drug offenders registered a stronger preference for prison than did white drug offenders. Conversely, in one third (9 of 30) of the racial comparisons, white drug offenders voiced a stronger preference for prison. In neither case were the comparisons significant, likely because of the reduced number of cases when we controlled for drug offenses. Taken as a whole, then, it appears that racial differences in perceptions of the severity of sanctions persisted when we controlled for drug convictions, although they may have been attenuated because Blacks and Whites who were convicted of drug offenses shared similar concerns about drug testing and being revoked.

Similarly, a larger percentage of black respondents than white respondents had experienced EM, which may have influenced their willingness to serve alternatives. We first compared all those with experience with EM (n = 37) with all those who had no such experience (n = 66); 10 respondents did not answer the question. We found that for 26 of 30 comparisons, the respondents with no experience with EM were willing to serve more of each alternative than were those with experience with that alternative, and 13 of those comparisons achieved significance (p < .05). Regarding the impact of having had experience with EM on a preference for prison over alternatives, respondents who had experience with EM were significantly more likely to be willing to serve some duration of EM again than were those with no such experience. Perhaps those with experience with EM were more likely to try it again because they learned how to avoid some of the pitfalls of close supervision. But this finding holds only for the comparison between EM and prison. Prior experience with EM had no consistent or significant impact on a respondent's willingness to serve a prison sentence over the various other alternatives considered here.

We then looked for racial differences in perceptions of the severity of sanctions, controlling for experience with EM. When comparing Blacks (n = 22) and Whites (n = 15) who had previous experience with EM, we found that the results closely mirrored those from the general sample. Whites were willing to serve more of each alternative than were Blacks in 22 of 30 comparisons (again three duration indices for each of 10 sanctions), and 10 of these comparisons achieved statistical significance. Blacks also registered a stronger preference for prison than did Whites in 23 out of 30 comparisons. Again, partly because of the sample size, few of the differences achieved significance, but those that did were in the expected direction. Of the few comparisons that showed that Blacks were willing to serve longer durations or that Whites preferred prison, none achieved statistical significance.

Similar to the results generated when we controlled for a drug offense, racial differences in perceptions of the severity of sanctions persisted when we controlled for EM, although they may have been slightly attenuated because Blacks and Whites now shared the EM experience and perhaps similar concerns about the "gamble" of serving alternatives. When we controlled for a drug offense, the racial difference remained in 46 of 60 possible comparisons, and when we controlled for experience with EM, the racial difference remained in 45 of 60 possible comparisons. In sum, when we accounted for the only recorded differences between the black and white samples, the results did not contradict those presented in Tables 4.2–4.4. Racial differences persisted, although they may have been slightly reduced.

Clearly, larger samples are needed to determine whether these findings are robust. If racial differences in having a drug conviction or experience serving EM do not account for the observed racial differences in perceptions of the severity of sanctions, why were Blacks more likely than Whites to choose prison instead of an alternative sanction, and why were they unwilling to serve as much of each alternative sanction? As we suggested earlier, there are at least two possible explanations. Either Blacks truly view prison as less punitive than alternatives, or Blacks view alternatives as too much of a gamble and their "risk assessment" of alternatives encourages them to choose prison, rather than entertain a high perceived risk of revocation by gambling on an alternative. Although our study does not speak to this issue directly, we did present respondents with a variety of reasons for avoiding alternative sanctions and asked them how important each reason was.

In Table 4.5, we present racial differences in how important various reasons were for avoiding alternative sanctions. Compared to white respondents, black respondents were more likely to identify each of the eight reasons posed as a "very important" reason for avoiding alternatives. Compared to Blacks, Whites were more likely to say that each of the eight reasons was "not at all important." Over half (55.6%) of the black respondents and 44.4% of white respondents agreed that a "very important reason" to avoid alternatives is that if you fail to complete the alternative, you end up back in prison, and it is not surprising that this was the most important reason to avoid alternative sanctions cited by both Whites and Blacks. But compared to only 20.4% of Whites, 43.6% of Blacks said that a "very important reason" for avoiding alternatives is that officers are too hard on participants; they try to catch them and revoke them back to prison. More than one in three (38.9%) Blacks (compared to only 18.9% of Whites) said that a "very important reason" to avoid alternative sanctions is that inmates are abused by officers who oversee the programs. Compared to white respondents (39.6%), over half of the black respondents (55.6%) said that a "very important" or "pretty important" reason for avoiding alternatives is that serving time in prison is less of a hassle; the programs have too many responsibilities. One in three (37%) black respondents, compared to 24.5% of Whites, said that a "very important" or "pretty important" reason was that "in general, living in prison is easier than living outside prison."

Table 4.5  Reasons Why Probationers Would Avoid an
Alternative Sanction by Race (Percentages)

| Reasons to Avoid the Sanction | Very important | | Pretty important | | Somewhat important | | Not at all important | |
|---|---|---|---|---|---|---|---|---|
| | White | Black | White | Black | White | Black | White | Black |
| Programs like these are too hard to complete | 14.8 | 20.0 | 24.1 | 20.0 | 27.8 | 30.9 | 33.3 | 29.1 |
| Program rules are too hard to follow | 13.0 | 29.1 | 20.4 | 23.6 | 25.9 | 12.7 | 40.7 | 34.5 |
| Officers are too hard on the program participants, they try to catch them and send them back to prison | 20.4 | 43.6 | 13.0 | 10.9 | 18.5 | 16.4 | 48.1 | 29.1 |
| Serving time in prison is easier than the alternatives offered by DOC | 22.2 | 30.9 | 24.1 | 18.2 | 22.2 | 21.8 | 31.5 | 29.1 |
| If you fail to complete the alternative, you end up back in prison | 44.4 | 55.6 | 24.1 | 18.5 | 11.1 | 13.0 | 20.4 | 13.0 |
| In general, living in prison is easier than living outside prison | 13.2 | 25.9 | 11.3 | 11.1 | 22.6 | 20.4 | 52.8 | 42.6 |
| Inmates are abused by parole and probation officers who oversee the programs | 18.9 | 38.9 | 17.0 | 14.8 | 22.6 | 18.5 | 41.5 | 27.8 |
| Serving time in prison is less hassle, the programs have too many responsibilities | 22.6 | 35.2 | 17.0 | 20.4 | 18.9 | 14.8 | 41.5 | 29.6 |

As can be seen in Table 4.5, racial differences are significant at the .05 level for three items: "Program rules are too hard to follow," "Officers are too hard on the program participants; they try to catch them and send them back to prison," and "Inmates are abused by parole and probation officers who oversee the programs." Black respondents were significantly more likely to feel that program rules, and personnel who administer the alternative sanctions, make completing the alternatives difficult, This finding implies that Blacks perceive a greater risk of revocation associated with alternatives than do Whites, and we suggest that this higher risk assessment makes them less willing to gamble on alternatives and more likely to choose prison instead.

# Racial Differences in Rankings of the Severity of Sanctions

Blacks and Whites in our sample differed in their willingness to participate in alternative sanctions, in their preference for prison over alternatives, and in the amount of these alternatives they were willing to serve. But how did these racial differences influence rankings of the relative punitiveness of a range of sanctions, including prison? Extrapolating from the results presented in the previous tables, we produced racial differences in the rankings of the punitiveness of alternative sanctions and prison. In Table 4.6, these rankings are presented by race and for each imprisonment-duration index (4, 8, and 12 months), with the most-punitive sanctions at the top of the table and the least-punitive sanctions at the bottom.

Among the most consistent findings were that both Blacks and Whites perceived that county jail and boot camp were the most punitive sanctions for each duration index and that regular probation was the least severe. It is interesting that black respondents consistently perceived boot camp to be more severe than county jail, while Whites consistently perceived county jail to be more severe than boot camp. Blacks may have perceived boot camp as too controlling, with a high risk of revocation, while Whites may have viewed it as a physically safer environment than county jail.

For each duration index, Whites ranked prison as the third most punitive sanction behind county jail and boot camp and ranked day reporting, community service, and regular probation as the least punitive sanction. Among Whites, between prison (the third most punitive) and day reporting (the ninth most punitive), the five sanctions of ISP, day fine, EM, halfway house, and intermittent incarceration circulated between fourth and eighth in the rankings of punitiveness. In general, Whites' rankings of the punitiveness of sanctions appear relatively stable, regardless of the duration index. The most obvious racial difference was how Blacks and Whites ranked the punitiveness of prison compared to the other sanctions.

As we noted earlier, within each duration index, Whites ranked prison as the third most-punitive sanction behind county jail and boot camp. However, Blacks ranked prison seventh, ninth, and tenth in relative severity in the 4, 8, and 12-months indices, respectively. We suspect that as the proposed dura-

Table 4.6  Ranking of Sanction Punitiveness, Blacks v. Whites

| Severity Continuum | 4 Months Index | | 8 Months Index | | 12 Months Index | |
|---|---|---|---|---|---|---|
| | Black | White | Black | White | Black | White |
| Most Punitive | Boot Camp | County Jail | Boot Camp | County Jail | Boot Camp | County Jail |
| | County Jail | Boot Camp | County Jail | Boot Camp | County Jail | Boot Camp |
| | Day Fine | Prison | Day Fine | Prison | Elec. Monitor. | Prison |
| | Elec. Monitor. | ISP | Elec. Monitor. | Halfway House | Day Fine | Day Fine |
| | ISP | Day Fine | ISP | ISP | ISP | Elec. Monitor. |
| | Inter. Incarcer. | Elec. Monitor. | Halfway House | Day Fine | Halfway House | Inter. Incarcer. |
| | Prison | Inter. Incarcer. | Inter. Incarcer. | Elec. Monitor. | Inter. Incarcer. | Halfway House |
| | Halfway House | Halfway House | Day Report. | Inter. Incarcer. | Day Report. | ISP |
| | Day Report. | Day Report. | Prison | Day Report. | Comm. Service | Comm. Service |
| | Comm. Service | Comm. Service | Comm. Service | Comm. Service | Prison | Day Report. |
| Least Punitive | Reg. Probat. | Reg. Probat. | Reg. Probat. | Reg. Probat. | Reg. Probat. | Reg. Probat. |

tion of imprisonment to be avoided increased, Blacks' "risk assessment" of alternatives grew, and they became less willing to gamble on serving an alternative that might result in their revocation back to prison to serve out the entire term. Blacks were willing to serve only incrementally more of the alternative when they considered 4, then 8, and then 12 months of incarceration because as time spent in an alternative increases, so does the perceived likelihood of mistreatment, discrimination, and harassment from program officers. This dynamic pushed the severity of prison down from 7th to 9th and finally to 10th in the rankings of punitiveness in Table 4.6. In the 8-months imprisonment index, only community service and regular probation were viewed as less punitive than prison. When considering 12 months of imprisonment, Blacks ranked 9 of the 10 alternative sanctions as more punitive than prison, with only regular probation ranked as less severe than incarceration.

# Discussion

Spelman (1995) and Crouch (1993) claimed that, compared to Whites, Blacks are more likely to choose prison over probation. We investigated if this was the case among our sample of probationers and across a range of alternatives, and asked the question, if so, why? We found that black probationers were more likely than Whites to refuse to participate in alternative sanctions, that Blacks were more likely than Whites to choose imprisonment over alternatives, and that, among offenders who were willing to serve alternatives to avoid prison, Whites would serve longer durations of them. Additionally, 20–25% of black respondents would choose prison rather than serve any duration of time in county jail, boot camp, EM, day reporting, ISP, or intermittent incarceration, and over a third of Blacks would choose prison rather than serve any duration of day fine. Blacks are approximately two to four times as likely as Whites to choose prison rather than participate in a given alternative sanction.

Black probationers evidence significantly more concern about participating in alternatives than do Whites. These concerns center on program rules that are difficult to follow and mistreatment at the hands of parole and probation officers and other personnel who oversee the alternative sanctions—both of which may increase the risk of revocation. Blacks seem to view alternative sanctions as more of a gamble than do Whites, and although our findings do not specifically address the issue, it is possible that Blacks see alternative sanction programs as biased against them. At this stage, it is unclear whether the relative perceived "ease" of prison is the primary factor in the observed racial differences or if Blacks simply calculate a higher risk assessment of alternatives and are less willing to gamble on them. Future work should address this issue.

The assumption that a brief prison term is more punitive and more likely to be a deterrent than are alternative sanctions was not supported in our work, and our findings build on the findings of others who have studied offenders' perceptions of the severity of criminal sanctions. The results also point to racial differences in rational choice/deterrence processes associated with criminal sanctions, particularly if, as suggested, Blacks produce a difference risk assessment of prison versus alternatives than do Whites. But the idea that Blacks and Whites evaluate these sanctions differently and are therefore likely to react to them differently has not been examined in any depth. As Wood and Grasmick (1999, p. 22) noted, the issue "bears directly on a 'rational' evaluation of costs and benefits by each potential offender."

Our results suggest that a brief prison term may be more of a deterrent for Whites than for Blacks, since black probationers' rankings of nearly all alternatives as more punitive than prison "inverts the penal code's hierarchy of sanctions thought to control crime" (Crouch, 1993, p. 86). These findings bring into question the deterrent value of brief imprisonment, particularly for Blacks, and suggest that some offenders may experience alternatives as either more punitive than previously suspected or more of a gamble with a higher likelihood of revocation—encouraging many to choose prison instead.

The findings revealed statistically significant racial differences with regard to the punitiveness of imprisonment compared to alternatives, willingness to participate in such sanctions, and rankings of the severity of sanctions. Although offenders perceive differences in the severity of sanctions, the calculus seems different for Blacks and Whites. But our research had several obvious limitations that deserve to be mentioned. Our work presented in this chapter is plainly exploratory, and because we had only a small number of cases, we did not present multivariate analyses to examine the importance of race when other sociodemographic or experiential factors that may influence how offenders perceive the punitiveness of sanctions are controlled. In addition, all our respondents were from one urban, Midwestern community. A larger data collection effort is needed to determine whether racial differences found here can be generalized to other jurisdictions.

It is also not possible for us to state conclusively what caused these racial differences. At least three dynamics may be operational: 1) Blacks perceive prison as less punitive than Whites and are therefore more likely to choose prison than are Whites, regardless of issues related to alternatives; 2) Blacks perceive alternatives as too much of a hassle compared to prison, with abusive program officers and rules that are too hard to follow; and 3) Blacks perceive a significantly higher risk of revocation associated with alternatives than do Whites, which increases the "gamble" of participating in them. These three dynamics may operate in tandem to generate the racial differences found in our study, although which is the most influential remains uncertain.

Crouch (1993) points out that offenders' perceptions of sanctions have likely changed over the past two decades due to the implementation of prison reforms. On the one hand, harsher prison sentences due to mandatory sentencing and Truth-In-Sentencing legislation may have increased the perceived punitiveness of prison. On the other hand, litigated prison reforms to reduce overcrowding and abusive conditions and to provide more prison programs may have reduced the perceived punitiveness of prisons—particularly among offenders with substantial experience in the correctional system. It is also true that new surveillance technologies have improved the ability to supervise offenders in the community, and may have increased the perceived likelihood of revocation among offenders, and thus the harshness of alternatives. These factors suggest that a rise in the number and variety of alternatives, and structural changes in the manner in which criminal justice punishments are delivered, may influence how offenders perceive the punitiveness of a range of sanctions. It seems likely, therefore, that offenders' rankings of sanction severity have changed over time and will continue to change in response to prison reforms. As such, there are a number of fruitful avenues for research on this topic.

# Gender Differences in Exchange Rates

Just as Blacks differ from Whites in their willingness to engage in alternative sanctions, it is quite possible that males may differ from females in much the same way. Nevertheless, until we began the exploration into exchange rates, no research of which we were aware examined gender differences in the amount of time offenders would serve in the community to avoid prison. We began that exploration with a sample of Oklahoma prisoners and continued that effort with the sample of Indiana probationers described above and, later, Kentucky probationers and parolees. We thus begin this section with a thorough discussion of gender differences in exchange rates among the Oklahoma prisoners (the first and most detailed analysis we conducted) then close the chapter with supporting evidence from the Indiana and Kentucky samples.

In Table 4.7, we display some basic descriptive information about the inmate respondents from Oklahoma. Overall, the inmate respondents from Oklahoma had served an average of one year and nine months total time in prisons, with males averaging two years three months and females averaging one year four months. The average duration of their longest single prison stay was about 15 months. The inmates averaged 33 years of age and just over 11 years education. Nearly 80% of female inmates and 65.7% of males had at least one child. Despite this high rate of parenthood, only 23.4% of males and 19.3% of females were currently married. In sum, the inmates in the study represent the kind of offenders' most likely eligible for participation in a range of alternative sanctions. As noted previously, just over half our data came from female inmates and Oklahoma registered the highest rate of female incarceration in the United States at the time of the study. The high proportion of female inmates allowed us to examine gender differences in ranking the punitiveness of criminal sanctions.

Table 4.7  Descriptive Statistics of the Oklahoma Inmate Sample,
Men and Women

|  | Men | Women | All Respondents |
|---|---|---|---|
| Number of Cases* | 181 | 224 | 415 |
| Average Age | 34 | 32 | 33 |
| Average Years Education | 11.34 | 11.31 | 11.32 |
| Marital Status: Percentages (Ns) |  |  |  |
| Single, Never Married | 36.0(63) | 38.1(83) | 37.2(147) |
| Single, Divorced or Separated | 39.4(69) | 37.6(82) | 38.2(151) |
| Currently Married | 23.4(41) | 19.3(42) | 21.0(83) |
| Widowed (Spouse died) | 1.1(2) | 5.0(11) | 3.5(14) |
| R has at least one child | 65.7(119) | 79.5(178) | 71.8(298) |
| Total time in all prisons: |  |  |  |
| Median | 2 years, | 1 year, | 1 year, |
|  | 3 months | 4 months | 9 months |
| Longest single prison stay: |  |  |  |
| Median | 1 year, | 1 year, | 1 year, |
|  | 4 months | 3 months | 3 months |

* The sum of the men and women does not equal 415 respondents because 10 respondents did not state their gender.

The percent of male and female inmates who will refuse to participate in a given sanction to avoid serving 4, 8, and 12-months actual imprisonment are displayed in Table 4.8. The results presented in the table reveal that women were more willing to participate in alternatives than were men. The gender difference was most evident with regard to Boot Camp, Regular Probation, Community Service, ISP, Intermittent Incarceration, and Day Fine, with women registering markedly lower refusal rates than men for these sanctions. The pattern of women being more amenable to alternatives held with the exception of Electronic Monitoring and Halfway House, in which case women were less willing to participate.

This discrepancy may be a function of the restrictions associated with the sanctions. For example, the description of Halfway House presented to the inmates stated that no visitors were allowed—a restriction that would preclude mothers from living with their children or bringing them to the House. In the case of Electronic Monitoring—an incapacitating punishment designed to restrict physical movement—women may demand greater flexibility in their schedules to attend to the needs of children. The requirements of electronic mon-

Table 4.8  Percentages of Male v. Female Inmates who will not participate in the Specified Alternative Sanction to Avoid 4, 8, and 12 Months of Medium-Security Imprisonment (Number of Inmates Refusing in Parentheses)

|  | 4 | 8 | 12 |
|---|---|---|---|
| County Jail |  |  |  |
| Male | 30.4 (55) | 19.9 (36) | 16.0 (29) |
| Female | 27.7 (62) | 19.6 (44) | 21.4 (48) |
| Boot Camp |  |  |  |
| Male | 36.5 (62) | 29.3 (53) | 26.0 (47) |
| Female | 25.0 (56) | 20.1 (45) | 21.4 (48) |
| Electronic Monitoring |  |  |  |
| Male | 19.3 (35) | 11.0 (20) | 13.3 (24) |
| Female | 22.8 (51) | 16.5 (37) | 15.2 (34) |
| Regular Probation |  |  |  |
| Male | 27.1 (49) | 17.7 (32) | 14.4 (26) |
| Female | 14.3 (32) | 10.3 (23) | 10.3 (23) |
| Community Service |  |  |  |
| Male | 19.3 (35) | 13.8 (25) | 12.2 (22) |
| Female | 8.5 (19) | 8.5 (19) | 7.1 (16) |
| Day Reporting |  |  |  |
| Male | 21.5 (39) | 17.7 (32) | 18.2 (33) |
| Female | 17.9 (40) | 13.8 (31) | 13.4 (30) |
| Intensive Supervision Probation |  |  |  |
| Male | 29.8 (54) | 24.9 (45) | 21.5 (39) |
| Female | 23.2 (52) | 17.9 (40) | 17.9 (40) |
| Intermittent Incarceration |  |  |  |
| Male | 18.8 (34) | 15.5 (28) | 14.4 (26) |
| Female | 12.1 (27) | 8.5 (19) | 8.9 (20) |
| Halfway House |  |  |  |
| Male | 8.8 (16) | 6.6 (12) | 6.6 (12) |
| Female | 9.4 (21) | 7.1 (15) | 6.7 (15) |
| Day Fine |  |  |  |
| Male | 35.9 (65) | 31.5 (57) | 30.9 (56) |
| Female | 24.1 (54) | 21.0 (47) | 19.6 (44) |

itoring may be viewed as too restrictive by many women given the unpredictable nature of childcare and supervision. With the exception of these two sanctions, women were more willing to participate in alternative sanctions than were men, though it is apparent that men and women shared a similar dislike of county jail and a high rate of acceptance of halfway house.

The results presented in Table 4.8 demonstrate that in general, women were more amenable to alternative sanctions than were men—that is, a larger proportion of women said they were willing to participate in most of the alternatives examined here. However, this finding alone is not sufficient to determine if women rate sanctions the same as men with respect to prison. Findings presented in Table 4.9 allow such a comparison.

The results presented in Table 4.9 display gender differences in exchange rates for the sample of Oklahoma prisoners willing to serve any amount of the sanction. The pattern of gender differences was very similar to that displayed in Table 4.8. For every sanction except Halfway House, women were willing to endure more of the alternative sanction than men to avoid a specific duration of actual imprisonment. For example, to avoid 4 months imprisonment, women would serve an average of .56 months more County Jail (p < .05), 92 more hours of Community Service, and over a month more Electronic Monitoring than men. Though nearly 23% of women refused to participate in Electronic Monitoring to avoid 4 months imprisonment, those who were willing to serve the sanction would do significantly more than men (p < .05). Regarding gender differences, only in the case of Halfway House would women do less of the alternative than men, a finding that may be explained by the restrictive "no visitors" description discussed earlier. This restriction may have caused a larger percentage of women to refuse participation and may be the reason why women would endure less Halfway House than men. Clearly more research focusing on the unique needs of female inmates is required; particularly if it is established that female inmates are more amenable to alternative sanctions than are men.

Perhaps the most striking feature of Table 4.9 is the level of agreement between male and female inmates regarding the relative punitiveness of sanctions. The male and female rankings under the "4 Months Index" column and the "12 Months Index" column were identical, and the rankings under the "8 Months Index" column differ only marginally. Using the "4 Months Index," only Boot Camp and County Jail were rated more severe than prison. But the punitiveness of prison declined markedly when moving to the 8 and 12-month indices, where men rated prison as the 8th most punitive sanction, and women rated prison as the 6th and 8th most punitive, respectively.

The results presented in Table 4.9 also reveal that the increased uncertainty of completing alternatives over longer periods of time pushed the perceived punitiveness of "alternatives" up the severity scale, while imprisonment—as a known and predictable punishment—declined to the point where it was rated

Table 4.9  Average Amount of Alternative Sanctions Inmates
Would Be Willing to Serve to Avoid 4, 8, and 12 Months of
Medium-Security Imprisonment: Males v. Females
(Alternative Sanction Unit of Analysis in Parentheses)

|  | 4 months | 8 months | 12 months |
|---|---|---|---|
| County Jail (Months) | | | |
| Male | 2.68 | 3.67 | 4.74 |
| Female | 3.24** | 4.27** | 5.50** |
| Boot Camp (Months) | | | |
| Male | 2.65 | 3.45 | 4.39 |
| Female | 2.79 | 3.92** | 4.99** |
| Electronic Monitoring (Months) | | | |
| Male | 5.29 | 7.75 | 10.03 |
| Female | 6.40** | 8.40 | 10.95** |
| Regular Probation (Years) | | | |
| Male | 2.74 | 3.17 | 3.59 |
| Female | 2.93 | 3.67* | 4.68** |
| Community Service (Hours) | | | |
| Male | 554 | 772 | 1039 |
| Female | 646 | 904* | 1286** |
| Day Reporting (Months) | | | |
| Male | 4.44 | 6.35 | 7.93 |
| Female | 4.71 | 6.56 | 8.30 |
| Intensive Supervision Probation (Months) | | | |
| Male | 5.71 | 8.44 | 10.73 |
| Female | 5.90 | 8.41 | 11.45 |
| Intermittent Incarceration (Days) | | | |
| Male | 82 | 122 | 151 |
| Female | 88 | 126 | 161* |
| Halfway House (Months) | | | |
| Male | 5.00 | 7.28 | 9.23 |
| Female | 4.91 | 6.99 | 8.55 |
| Day Fine (Days) | | | |
| Male | 82 | 114 | 137 |
| Female | 83 | 112 | 141 |

* p < .05
** p < .01
*** p < .001

**Table 4.10  Average Amount of Alternative Sanctions Kentucky Probationers and Parolees Would Be Willing to Serve to Avoid 12 Months of Medium-Security Imprisonment: Males v. Females**

| Sanction Type | Male (N = 467) | Female (N = 119) |
|---|---|---|
| County Jail | 5.41 | 6.06 |
| Boot Camp | 6.18 | 5.52 |
| Day Fine | 11.48 | 14.93* |
| Electronic Monitoring | 13.31 | 16.49* |
| Halfway House | 13.87 | 16.53* |
| Intermittent Incarceration | 14.21 | 16.08 |
| Day Reporting | 15.92 | 21.35** |
| Community Service# | 1786 | 1991 |
| Regular Probation | 22.84 | 26.29* |

* Difference in Mean Score Significant at p < .01(One-tailed Independent Sample t-tests using Levene's Test for Equality of Variances)
** Difference in Mean Score Significant at p < .001 (One-tailed Independent Sample t-tests using Levene's Test for Equality of Variances
# Community Service is measured in hours. We assigned offenders 20 hours per week, although very few offenders perform that amount of community service per week. If anything, our calculation inflated the punitiveness of community service.

more severe than only Regular Probation and Community Service by both men and women on the 12 month scale. The law of diminishing returns forces imprisonment toward the bottom of the punitiveness scale, making it a less punitive punishment compared to most alternatives.

In more recent efforts, we used data from probationers and parolees from Kentucky to determine whether these gender differences found among Oklahoma prisoners were repeated in other samples of offenders supervised in the community. The mean exchange rates for male and female Kentucky probationers and parolees are compared to 12 months medium-security imprisonment in Table 4.10.

The results presented in Table 4.10 suggest that males rated county jail as the most punitive sanction, with boot camp the second most punitive and probation and community service as the least punitive sanctions. Females, however, rated boot camp as the most severe sanction followed by county jail, but concurred that probation and community service were the least punitive sanctions. The results further indicate that, compared to females, males would serve fewer months of day fine, electronic monitoring, halfway house, day reporting, and regular probation to avoid 12 months in prison. As such, the

Table 4.11  Ranking of Sanction Punitiveness, Kentucky and Oklahoma,
Males and Females

| Severity Continuum | Kentucky | | Oklahoma | |
|---|---|---|---|---|
| | Male (N = 467) | Female (N = 119) | Male (181) | Female (224) |
| Most Punitive | County Jail | Boot Camp | Boot Camp | Day Fine |
| | Boot Camp | County Jail | Day Fine | Boot Camp |
| | Day Fine | Prison | County Jail | Intermittent Incarceration |
| | Prison | Day Fine | Intermittent Incarceration | County Jail |
| | Electronic Monitoring | Intermittent Incarceration | Day Reporting | Day Reporting |
| | Halfway House | Electronic Monitoring | Halfway House | Halfway House |
| | Intermittent Incarceration | Halfway House | Electronic Monitoring | Electronic Monitoring |
| | Day Reporting | Day Reporting | Prison | Prison |
| | Community Service | Community Service | Community Service | Community Service |
| Least Punitive | Regular Probation | Regular Probation | Regular Probation | Regular Probation |

findings among the Kentucky probationers and parolees support the gender differences in exchange rates found among the Oklahoma prisoners.

In Table 4.11, we compare the ranking of the correctional sanctions for Kentucky males and female probationers/parolees with those of the Oklahoma prisoners using responses regarding how much of these sanctions the respondents would endure to avoid 12 months incarceration in a medium-security facility. These findings present an interesting contrast. The most notable of the findings is that gender appears to have less impact than the type of sanction currently being served on the respondent's rating of the punitiveness of the alternative. Male and female respondents from Kentucky ranked county jail and boot camp as more punitive than prison and day reporting, community service, and regular probation as the least punitive sanctions. Among the Kentucky respondents, day fine was ranked as either more punitive than prison (males) or slightly less punitive than prison (females), with electronic monitoring, halfway house, and intermittent incarceration ranked closely thereafter as less punitive than prison but more punitive than day reporting. Oklahoma respondents, on the other hand, also ranked boot camp and county jail as much more punitive than prison, but also felt that, with the exception of community service and regular probation, prison was less punitive than all other community sanctions. In Chapter 5, we discuss the fact that one of our more consistent findings across independent samples and locations is that imprisonment experience reduces the perceived severity of imprisonment relative to other sanctions. For this reason, because *all* Oklahoma respondents are inmates and had imprisonment experience (compared to approximately half of the Kentucky respondents), the effect of this differential in the two samples' relative experience with imprisonment serves to generate a higher average severity ranking for prison in the Kentucky sample, and a lower average severity ranking for prison in the Oklahoma sample. We suspect that if all Kentucky respondents had experience with imprisonment, their average severity ranking of prison would more closely approximate that of the Oklahoma inmate sample.

# Summary of Gender Differences in Exchange Rates

As noted in the introduction, previous research has ignored gender differences. The samples of female inmates and probationers and parolees in our sample provide the first look at gender differences in how offenders rank the severity of alternatives compared to prison. With the rapid rise in female offender populations at the end of the 20th century, examination of female perceptions of sanction severity would seem warranted. If women are significantly more amenable to such sanctions, their enrollment might be increased, saving prison space and financial resources.

The observed gender differences in perceived punitiveness of sanctions suggest gender differences in deterrence dynamics—particularly with regard to informal costs of imprisonment. Recall that our findings indicate that women were more amenable to alternatives and would do more time in alternatives than will men. Women in the Oklahoma sample averaged 32 years of age and nearly 80% of them had at least one child. At the same time over 75% of these female inmates claim to be single. We assume that single women with children typically take primary responsibility for care-giving in the home—particularly child care. Such care-giving is impossible if a woman is incarcerated, but remains likely if the woman is placed in a community-based alternative sanction. Further, single mothers who are sentenced to imprisonment may often lose custody of their children, while if placed in a community-based program they may not. We believe this is one reason why women are more amenable to alternative sanctions.

In addition, most states have far fewer prisons for female offenders than for males, and many have only one such prison. Women sentenced to imprisonment may find themselves far removed (geographically) from their home communities, and distance may preclude the possibility of regular contact with children and family members. This problem is not nearly as severe for men, who may manage to serve their time in prisons or county jails in or near their home communities, and who typically do not assume primary care-giving responsibilities.

Consequently, there may be at least two strong reasons why women view imprisonment as more punitive than alternatives compared to men. This implies that women may employ a different "cost-benefit analysis" than men when considering criminal behavior, pointing to a possible gender difference in deterrence dynamics. Women may be more tuned to the informal costs of imprisonment than are men, and if so, women with primary care-giving duties who face imprisonment may be ideal candidates for community-based sanctions. Our findings raise an interesting question—do deterrence dynamics differ by gender?

It seems clear that female inmates respond differently than males to alternative sanctions. While the two groups generate a similar punitiveness ranking with regard to specific punishments, women appear significantly more amenable to alternatives than do men and are willing to endure longer durations of those alternatives. We suggest that gender differences in the rational-choice calculation of costs and benefits are likely to exist, and these differences may influence gender differences in deterrence dynamics. Such potential gender differences have been ignored by rational choice and deterrence scholars, but there seems evidence in their favor. Women are particularly likely to be influenced by care-giving responsibilities and correction systems offer them fewer geographic options for incarceration. Consideration of the unique needs of female inmates—particularly those with primary care-giving responsibilities —should be a primary research focus in sanction development.

# Conclusion

Our work reveals statistically significant differences in opinions of Blacks and Whites and males and females with regard to the severity of imprisonment compared to alternatives, as well as their willingness to participate in such sanctions. Mauer (1999) calls for increased use of alternative sanctions to reduce costs and improve the chances of re-integration into the community.

Nevertheless, he argues that, in some jurisdictions, white offenders are more likely to participate in alternative sanctions than are Blacks, while Blacks continue to receive prison terms in large numbers. We expect that a similar finding would hold true for males and females. Mauer goes on to argue that alternative sanction programs should be monitored to ensure that African-American and Hispanic offenders are appropriately represented in these sanctions, since they offer the best chances for treatment, education, and employment. If it is true that minorities are under-represented in alternatives, it may be attributed in part to the reputation these alternatives have among Blacks (and possibly Hispanics), and to their greater preference for prison compared to Whites. It seems likely, therefore, that the perception many Blacks hold of a biased and abusive criminal justice system translates to suspicion regarding alternatives, since a much higher proportion of Blacks compared to Whites would rather serve their prison sentences than risk investing time and effort in an alternative with a strong perceived likelihood of mistreatment and revocation. Until this perception (whether real or imagined) is changed, alternative sanctions will remain more attractive to Whites, and the race difference in perceptions of sanction severity will persist.

A similar dynamic may exist with regard to gender. It appears that the "pains of imprisonment" may be greater for females than males, making a prison sentence more punitive for females than males. As such, the continuum of sanctions may not only be different than Morris and Tonry first imagined it may also be dependent on the race and gender of the individual considering that continuum. We return to this discussion in the concluding chapters of this book.

# Notes

The results presented in Tables 4.2 and 4.4 include responses from those who stated that they would refuse to participate in any duration of an alternative sanction. Represented in Table 4.3, these respondents included all those who scored a 0 when asked how much of an alternative they would do to avoid 4, 8, or 12 months of actual imprisonment. The decision to include or exclude these respondents had a significant impact on the calculation of the ranking of the severity of sanctions (see Table 4.6). The inclusion of respondents who would refuse to do any duration of a sanction reduced the average number of months that both Blacks and Whites would serve to avoid a specified duration of imprisonment, since these respondents answered 0 to the question. However, the exclusion of 0 scores would inflate the perceived severity of prison by excluding all respondents who refused to serve an alternative to avoid imprisonment.

We included these 0 scores in our calculation of punishment equivalencies for several reasons. First, because a significant proportion of the respondents would choose imprisonment, rather than any duration of an alternative, this fact should be reflected in a ranking of the severity of sanctions because these respondents clearly viewed some alternatives as more punitive than imprisonment. Second, we defer to Greene's (2000) work on the problems associated with censored variables. Eliminating the 0 values results in a truncated distribution, which will produce biased coefficients in regression and necessarily must have the same effect on any lower-level statistics, such as means and percentages. What happens is similar to what would happen, for example, in a fear-of-crime study. The elimination of all respondents who were not fearful before calculating average fear of crime scores would bias the results. Censoring the equivalency measures would result in skewing all punishment equivalencies in a specific direction. As Greene (2000) pointed out, "the censoring of a range of values of the variable of interest introduces a distortion into conventional statistical results similar to that of truncation, presumably, if they were not censored, the data would be a representative sample from the population of interest" (p. 896).

Nevertheless, we conducted an additional analysis to examine how punishment equivalencies and the ranking of the severity of sanctions would change if persons who refused to do any amount of an alternative were excluded. The censoring of 0 scores had several obvious and predictable consequences. As expected, with the removal of the 0 scores, the average amounts of alternatives that the respondents are willing to serve increased across the board. However, racial differences exhibited the same pattern, with Whites willing to serve more of each alternative. In addition, these differences remained statistically significant, so there was no change in the pattern of racial differences noted in Table 5.4. The exclusion of 0 scores had an impact on racial differences in the ranking of the severity of sanctions shown in Table 5.6. Specifically, when 0 scores were excluded, the Blacks' rankings of the severity of prison increased from the 7th most punitive to the 5th most punitive in the "4 Months Index" and to the 6th most punitive in the 8 and 12-months indices (up from 9th and 10th most punitive, respectively). The Whites' ranking remained the same, with prison ranked 3rd most punitive within each duration index. With the 0 scores removed, Blacks appeared willing to serve more of each alternative, which bumped prison higher up the severity ranking, primarily because a much greater proportion of Blacks than of Whites refused to do any duration of each alternative (in other words, there were more 0s scored by Blacks than by Whites). However, as we noted earlier, the exclusion of 0 scores would serve to inflate the perceived severity of prison and reduce the perceived severity of alternatives.

# CHAPTER 5

# PRISON EXPERIENCE AND DIFFERENCES IN EXCHANGE RATES

In this chapter, we use data from probationers and parolees in Kentucky discussed earlier in Chapter 3 to examine whether correctional experience impacts perceptions of sanctions. Refer to Table 3.8 for the descriptive of this sample.

The results provided in Table 5.1 represent punishment equivalencies (exchange rates) that reflect the average number of months of an alternative that the Kentucky probationers and parolees were willing to serve to avoid 12 months of medium-security imprisonment and mirror those presented in Table 3.9 earlier. Responses were then compared by prison experience—in other words, responses from those offenders who had served time in prison were compared with those who had not to determine if the experience of prison impacted an offender's view of its punitiveness.

As discussed in Chapter 3, of the nine alternative sanctions presented, only county jail and boot camp were evaluated as more punitive than prison by the entire sample. To avoid 12 months of imprisonment, respondents were willing to serve an average of only 5.55 and 6.07 months of county jail and boot camp, respectively. They were willing to serve an average of more than 12 months of all other alternatives, although day fine was scored almost the same as prison (12.22 months) by the entire sample (in effect, a 1:1 exchange rate for day fines and prison). Regarding the least punitive alternatives, respondents were willing to serve an average of 23.56 months of regular probation and 22.82 months of community service (this total is derived by dividing 1825.86 hours by 20 hours per week based on four weeks per month) to avoid one year in prison (an exchange rate of approximately 2:1 for both sanctions over prison). Finally, respondents were willing to serve an average of 17.01 months of day reporting to avoid 12 months of prison (an exchange rate of approximately 1.4:1 for day reporting over prison).

Table 5.1  Amount of Alternative Sanction Offender Will Serve
to Avoid 12 Months in State Prison

| Sanction Type | Total Sample (N=588) | Never Served Time in Prison (N=300) | Has Served Time in Prison (N=269) |
|---|---|---|---|
| County Jail | 5.55 | 6.54** | 4.60 |
| Boot Camp | 6.07 | 7.46** | 4.65 |
| Day Fine | 12.22 | 13.84** | 10.45 |
| Electronic Monitoring | 13.95 | 16.42** | 11.33 |
| Halfway House | 14.42 | 16.14** | 12.77 |
| Intermittent Incarceration | 14.60 | 15.73* | 13.40 |
| Day Reporting | 17.01 | 18.37* | 15.53 |
| Community Service[a] | 1825.86 | 1894 | 1737 |
| Regular Probation | 23.56 | 26.00** | 21.00 |

* Difference in Mean Score Significant at $p<.01$ (One-tailed Independent Sample t-tests using Levene's Test for Equality of Variances)
** Difference in Mean Score Significant at $p<.001$ (One-tailed Independent Sample t-tests using Levene's Test for Equality of Variances)
a Community Service is measured in hours. We assigned offenders 20 hours per week, although very few offenders perform that amount of community service per week. If anything, our calculation inflated the punitiveness of community service.

In the remaining columns in Table 5.1, the mean responses are compared by incarceration experience utilizing one-tailed t-tests. The pattern uncovered using the entire sample holds with minor exceptions for the remaining columns when considering the 12-month index. Both those who have and those who have not been in prison rated county jail as the most punitive sanction, with boot camp the second most punitive and probation and community service as the least punitive sanctions (and far less punitive than prison). The rating of both boot camp and county jail as the most punitive alternative sanctions (and far more punitive than prison) matched findings presented earlier from both Oklahoma prisoners and Indiana probationers.

The results presented in Table 5.1 also indicate that, with the exception of community service where the direction of the association was the same but the difference did not reach statistical significance, for each alternative sanction, those who had served time in prison would do *less* of each alternative sanction to avoid 12 months in prison than those who had not served time in prison. Consequently, for practically all alternative sanctions, the exchange rate for the alternative sanction when compared to prison was lower for those

Table 5.2  Full OLS Models for Amount of Each Sanction Offenders Will Serve to Avoid 12 Months Imprisonment*

| Predictor | Community Service (N=517) | | Electronic Monitoring (N=517) | | Halfway House (N=516) | |
|---|---|---|---|---|---|---|
| | Beta | sig | Beta | sig | Beta | sig |
| Have Served Time in Prison | .042 | .176 | -.119 | .004 | -.101 | .015 |
| Black | -.170 | .000 | -.136 | .001 | -.085 | .029 |
| Age | -.174 | .000 | -.165 | .000 | -.096 | .018 |
| Male | -.031 | .231 | -.093 | .025 | -.085 | .025 |
| Reasons to Avoid Alternative Scale | -.155 | .000 | -.181 | .000 | -.055 | .113 |
| Reasons to Participate in Alternative Scale | .003 | .478 | .071 | .066 | .037 | .225 |
| Reasons to Avoid Prison Scale | .090 | .034 | -.031 | .262 | -.026 | .301 |
| $R^2$ /Adjusted $R^2$ | .088 | .075 | .137 | .126 | .052 | .039 |

* Community Service is measured in hours while Electronic Monitoring and Halfway House are measured in months. All models are estimated using one-tailed test of statistical significance.

who have served time in prison (and, to a lesser extent, for males) than their counterparts. These findings will be addressed in detail below.

We then used OLS regression to examine the impact of the predictor variables outlined above on the amount (in hours) of community service and the amount (in months) of electronic monitoring and halfway house that probationers and parolees would serve to avoid 12 months imprisonment. These results were presented in Table 3.10 earlier and discussed in detail in Chapter 3. For clarity, we have included those regression models here in Table 5.2. The findings presented in Table 5.2 indicated that, along with several other variables, previous incarceration in prison had a significant impact on the amount of both electronic monitoring and halfway house offenders were willing to serve to avoid 12 months in prison. Those who have served time in prison would endure significantly fewer months of electronic monitoring and halfway house to avoid 12 months in a medium-security prison.

Finally, we constructed a ranking that compares the perceived punitiveness of community service, electronic monitoring, halfway house, and six other

Table 5.3  Severity Ranking of Criminal Justice Sanctions
among Kentucky Probationers and Parolees

| Severity Ranking | All Respondents | No Prison Experience | Prison Experience |
|---|---|---|---|
| Most Severe | County Jail | County Jail | County Jail |
| | Boot Camp | Boot Camp | Boot Camp |
| | Prison | Prison | Day Fine |
| | Day Fine | Day Fine | Electronic Monitoring |
| | Electronic Monitoring | Intermittent Incarceration | Prison |
| | Halfway House | Halfway House | Halfway House |
| | Intermittent Incarceration | Electronic Monitoring | Intermittent Incarceration |
| | Day Reporting | Day Reporting | Day Reporting |
| | Community Service | Community Service | Regular Probation |
| Least Severe | Regular Probation | Regular Probation | Community Service |

sanctions to 12 months of imprisonment. Additionally, because the results suggest that experience with incarceration in prison is an important predictor of respondents' perceptions of the severity of at least one alternative sanction, we compare rankings of severity of alternative sanctions by that variable as well.

The results presented in Table 5.3 indicate that prison is not viewed by any group as the most severe sanction. For the entire sample and each subgroup, both boot camp and county jail are rated as more onerous than prison. Perhaps the most striking feature of this table concerns the ratings of the severity of prison among those offenders who have served time in prison. Offenders who have served time in prison view prison as the fifth most punitive sanction, ranked behind county jail, boot camp, day fine, and electronic monitoring. Additionally, the consistency of the rankings is readily apparent for respondents who have not been incarcerated in prison; they rank prison as the third most stringent sanction, with day reporting, community service, and regular probation rated as the three least stringent sanctions. Interestingly, those with prior prison experience were the only group not to rank regular probation as the least stringent alternative; this group perceived regular probation as a more stringent sanction than community service.

# Discussion

The results presented in this chapter suggest that prior prison experience registers a significant, negative association with exchange rates when comparing intermediate sanctions with imprisonment, and the influence of prior imprisonment remains for electronic monitoring and halfway house when controlling for other factors. Prior incarceration thus generally reduces the amount of the alternative offenders are willing to serve.

There are several possible reasons why prior imprisonment might influence exchange rates in this manner. Offenders with experience living in prison are less fearful of prison than those without such experience. For them, prison is less of an unknown and may even be viewed as easier than an intermediate sanction—particularly if they perceive the alternative as involving an unacceptable degree of intrusion, supervision, mistreatment, and/or a high likelihood of revocation. Fleisher (1995) notes that, "… prison isn't a risk that worries street hustlers. Things such as limited freedom, loss of privacy, violence, and variant sexual activity, which might frighten lawful citizens, don't frighten them" (p. 164). Particularly among inmates with experience serving time, imprisonment becomes familiar, while the outcome of involvement in alternatives is less certain and potentially more of a gamble.

Compared to living outside of prison, Morris and Tonry (1990) argue that:

> … many, though not all prisons, provide a safer and more comfortable environment than the environment from which many of our street criminals come. In prison, they are less likely to be assaulted or killed, they eat better, they often begin educational efforts they had previously entirely neglected, they sometimes begin to take hold of their lives and give them shape (p. 96).

Qualitative research provides further evidence to support these findings. This research suggests that offenders who have acquired knowledge and experience about living in prison appear less fearful of prison than those without such experience. Williams et al. (2008) suggest that once an inmate has served time in prison, prison is less of an unknown, and thus less likely to be feared. In much the same way that military boot camp is a daunting experience until a soldier has survived it, prison is an environment that many may dread until they have actually experienced it. After that initial incarceration experience, at least to some, prison may then be seen as easier than an alternative sanction—particularly if they perceive their sentence as unjust, unfair, or excessive, and are defiant toward that sentence as suggested above or they feel the community sanction has a high likelihood of revocation.

Among inmates with experience serving time, imprisonment becomes familiar; contrasted against an unfamiliar, unpredictable community sanction, these experienced offenders prefer the stability and predictability of the prison sentence to the alternative (whatever that may be). Persons without that same prior experience in prison may be more fearful of it, and will opt to do the alternative—and a longer duration of it—in order to avoid prison. As such, this finding calls into question the deterrent value of imprisonment, particularly because those who have served prison are more likely to choose prison over alternative sanctions compared to those with no prison experience (May et al., 2005).

Our own qualitative work supports these arguments. Over one in eight probationers and parolees we interviewed said that prison is easier than the alternative or that the alternatives were harder than prison. One in six responded that an offender can get out of prison quicker than if they served the alternative. Furthermore, one in ten said that the reason offenders would choose to serve prison time over an alternative was because they were afraid of getting into trouble and having the alternative revoked. Probationers and parolees also suggested that offenders would choose prison over an alternative because they "don't want to face their responsibilities," "they use prison to escape the rules of the alternative sanction," or "they do not want to deal with the probation officers" (Williams et al., 2008). Their comments, presented earlier, suggest that prison is not the most punitive sanction from their perspectives.

Qualitative work also indicates that among those with a history of imprisonment, intermediate sanctions may carry a sort of stigma. Based on the authors' interviews with offenders in a variety of settings, experienced cons often frown on offenders who volunteer for the intrusive supervision and restrictions of intermediate sanctions. For many older and more experienced offenders, then, willingness to serve an intermediate sanction may be seen as a "copout" of sorts, carrying a stigma of being reserved for younger and weaker inmates, and is to be avoided by those who have adapted to living in prison.

The pain of imprisonment can also be related to characteristics of the offender or the crime committed. It is true that those convicted of certain offenses (child molesters and rapists, for example) are often abused by other inmates, and first-timers generally have a tougher time than experienced cons. As noted by Morris and Tonry, what looks like an equal sentence of 12 months imprisonment, "... may, in practice, vary substantially in its impact on the offender" (1990, p. 102). One might expect, therefore, that the prison environment itself would generate an important contextual influence on penal exchange rates.

Among those with a history of imprisonment, intermediate sanctions may also carry a sort of stigma; this may be particularly true for older offenders. Based on the authors' interviews with offenders in other settings, some experienced cons view offenders who volunteer for the intrusive supervision and restrictions of intermediate sanctions as "punks" who are willing to subject themselves to "institutionalized embarrassment" at the hands of program officers and staff, and who are afraid to serve time in the general prison population. In fact, having been in prison may serve as a "status booster" particularly in inner cities where Petersilia and Turner (1990b) cite staff at the California Youth Authority and Department of Corrections who state that "... inmates steal the state-issued prison clothing to wear in the community because it lets everyone know they have done hard time" (p. 31). It is clear, then, that prior prison experience can have a significant impact on how one views the severity of both prison and alternatives.

Consistent with previous work, we determine that while some offenders may perceive imprisonment as the most punitive correctional sanction, this is not true for all or even most of them. Furthermore, as our findings demonstrated here, a number of offenders with prior prison experience (or who were currently on parole) chose to serve longer amounts of prison than alternative sanctions served in the community. These findings undermine classical deterrence doctrine that would claim that those who are imprisoned for a crime would be: a) less likely to re-offend and b) less likely to prefer prison over a community based sanction. Contrary to classical deterrence theory, offenders in prison or with prison experience were more likely to choose to do the time and be released, rather than "gamble" by investing time and effort in completing an alternative sanction with a high perceived likelihood of revocation, unacceptable restrictions, and supervision by hostile probation and parole officers.

The exchange rate evidence for offenders presented here, combined with the earlier findings presented in Chapter 3, suggest that reasons for avoiding or participating in alternative sanctions have little to do with either: a) an offender's prison experience or b) the specifics of the program or the institution in which inmates are serving time (i.e., program rules too strict, prison too harsh on inmates), but have more to do with the manner in which these programs are administered.  Perceptions of the inconvenience, intrusiveness, and punitiveness of intermediate sanctions seem to be strongly influenced by: a) the conduct and personalities of programmatic staff and parole/probation officers; b) high failure and revocation rates associated with many alternative sanctions; and c) how offenders subjectively rate the overall severity of prison compared to alternative sanctions. Consequently, the most important impacts on whether a person would choose to serve an alternative sanction in the community may have more to do with the people operating the program than the actual offender involved in the program or the program itself. If this is the case, then these findings would strengthen the conclusions of deterrence and rational choice scholars regarding the "indirect" sanctions or costs and the greater deterrent effect they have on recidivism (Grasmick and Bursik, 1990; and Williams & Hawkins, 1986).

# Conclusion

The findings presented here once again cast doubt on the value of prison as a crime reduction mechanism. Compared to those with no imprisonment history, offenders with prior prison experience would serve less of each alternative to avoid prison and voice a greater preference for prison rather than serve any duration of an alternative. Therefore, one might question the presumed deterrent value of brief imprisonment for some subgroups of offenders. The significance of our findings for rational choice/deterrence and social learning theories generates potentially provocative and controversial issues.

Our findings bear directly on issues associated with deterrence. The fact that inmates with prison experience view several alternatives as more punitive than prison brings into question the use of brief imprisonment as a specific deterrent. Findings presented here show that many inmates would rather serve a brief prison term than most of the alternatives, and many inmates view a brief prison term as an opportunity to recharge or relax away from the pressures of surviving on the street. Several inmates interviewed by the authors noted that the brief term they were to serve would give them the opportunity to have some dental work done at the expense of the state. Others appreciated the regular meals and shelter and a chance to "chill out" and see old friends. Clearly, a brief prison stay has little or no deterrent value for these persons, and such a sanction even has its attractive features for many offenders. For them, imprisonment is more predictable and less of a hassle than alternative sanctions.

Some readers may misconstrue our work as promoting alternatives over prison in order to achieve a greater reduction in recidivism or crime control. The efficacy of intermediate punishments compared to imprisonment is usually rated in terms of cost and crime prevention (i.e., recidivism). In fact, though most research on intermediate sanctions determines they are generally not more effective than imprisonment in reducing future crime, it is also the case that little evidence exists to suggest that imprisonment has a greater specific deterrent effect than intermediate sanctions. Additionally, while evaluations of intermediate sanctions note that such programs are not less effective than imprisonment, they are potentially less expensive than imprisonment. As noted by Tonry (1996), "… well managed intermediate sanctions offer a cost-effective way to keep [offenders] in the community at less cost than imprisonment and with no worse later prospect for criminality" (1996, p. 132). If an alternative sanction is equally effective (or ineffective) in reducing recidivism, perceived by offenders as equally punitive, and is significantly less expensive than imprisonment, there seems good reason to expand its use.

Our results also raise serious doubts about the validity of a continuum of sanctions bounded by regular probation at one extreme and traditional incarceration at the other. Though legislators and criminal justice policy-makers might prefer such an arrangement, and have operated under the assumption that such a continuum is valid, the reality appears more complex. Offenders with personal experience of both imprisonment and alternatives identify several alternatives as more punitive than prison. Depending on the specific sanction, a significant proportion of offenders prefer to participate in the alternative, even if it means a shorter duration of imprisonment. Consequently, our findings suggest a more complex decision-making process than that traditionally attributed to criminal offenders, who are uniquely aware of the pitfalls awaiting them should they enroll in certain alternatives. The conventional wisdom of placing regular probation at the low end of a continuum of sanction severity may be valid, but it seems clear many offenders perceive certain noncustodial sanctions as more onerous than traditional incarceration.

Along the same line, future researchers in this area should remain aware that offenders' self-reported perceptions may not always parallel their behaviors. That is, the sanction(s) respondents would prefer in a quantitative study such as our own, or in a more qualitative study, may or may not be indicative of what they would do if given an actual choice between custodial and noncustodial sentences.

We are aware of only one randomized field experiment in this regard, conducted by the Rand Corporation in Oregon. Given the choice, less than one in four convicted offenders (22.2%) chose to participate in an experiment that would have randomly assigned them to either prison or intensive supervision probation (Petersilia & Turner, 1990a; 1990b). Petersilia and Turner (1990b) cite Oregon officials who speculate that those who refused to participate in the experiment refused to do so because they "… may have been choosing the perceived less onerous sentence" (p. 31). Their research shows that, though difficult to implement, a study designed to explicitly compare expressed preferences with subsequent actual choices would contribute substantially to the body of literature on this topic. Our research was not designed to address this comparison directly, but nearly half of our respondents had served time in prison, thereby acquiring some experiential basis to evaluate noncustodial versus custodial sanctions.

As the popularity and application of alternative sanctions continues to grow, it behooves prosecutors, judges, and legislators to be cognizant of how offenders subjectively perceive the severity of prison when compared to alternative sanctions. By doing so, sentencing strategies based on valid and reliable exchange rates could be devised that would almost certainly decrease the burden placed on taxpayers to continue funding mass imprisonment, an investment that, to date, has provided far greater dividends at exacting retribution in the minds of policy-makers and the public than at dispensing fair, proportionate, or effective punishments.

# CHAPTER 6

# CRIMINAL JUSTICE PRACTITIONERS' AND THE PUBLIC'S VIEWS OF EXCHANGE RATES

In the previous chapters, we presented the history and use of exchange rates and relevant findings from offender populations about their attitudes and perceptions of the relative severity of correctional sanctions. In this chapter, we consider two other important populations whose opinions should be considered: practitioners in the criminal justice field and the general public. Because practitioners have a direct hand in both the sentencing (by judges) and the supervision (by probation and parole officers) of offenders under correctional supervision and because the public elects legislators who make laws regarding sentencing, the perceptions and attitudes of these groups about the punitiveness of various punishments are important. The use of alternatives is somewhat dependent on 1) judges' opinions of the severity of these sanctions and the reaction of the public to those sanctions and 2) the supervising officers' philosophy regarding community sanctions and their punitiveness (e.g., an officer who feels community sanctions are more punitive or effective may be less likely to return an offender guilty of technical violations to prison than one who feels community sanctions are less effective or punitive). Therefore, assessment of these groups' views of alternative sanctions is pivotal in the development of a more informed continuum of sanctions—if one even exists. As such, in this chapter, we explore judges', officers', and public perceptions of the relative severity of alternative sanctions compared to prison by examining punishment exchange rates generated by each group.

# Judges' Perceptions of Intermediate Sanctions

One population with a direct hand in the implementation of alternative sanctions is judges. A small number of studies have examined, both directly and indirectly, judges' attitudes and perceptions of alternatives. Finn (1984) examined judges' responses to prison overcrowding and determined that most judges cited that overcrowding was associated with the lack of money needed to support the expanded services related to probation and parole, as well as the building and maintaining of the required alternative facilities. Judges also acknowledged the pressure from strong public sentiment to lock away criminals. Cole, Mahoney, Thornton and Hanson (1988) explored judges' application and attitudes towards the use of fines and determined that judges were willing to use fines for more severe offenses. Lurigio (1987) examined the attitudes of judges and attorneys from Cook County Illinois concerning the use and implementation of intensive probation supervision (IPS). In that study, a number of judges were reluctant to use IPS and none of the judges reported that sentenced offenders chose prison instead of IPS (perhaps because of its relative infancy in that jurisdiction).

Wooldredge and Gordon (1997) used a random sample of 181 chief trial court judges to determine characteristics of the judiciary that would predict a greater use of alternatives as well as judges' willingness to use such sanctions. They determined that judges presiding in courts with less structured sentencing policies and longer minimum sentences were more likely to be amenable to using intermediate sanctions. The same was true for both smaller courts as well as courts with higher rates of plea bargaining. Judges also cited more structured sentencing policies as limiting their sentencing discretion and their ability to use alternative sanctions in lieu of prison (Wooldredge & Gordon 1997).

# Correctional Officials' Perceptions of Intermediate Sanctions

Most of the research on the perceptions of correctional officials revolves around victimization risk and role conflict (Gordon, Moriarty, & Grant, 2003; Kifer, Hemmens & Stohr, 2003). As such, little is known about the attitudes and beliefs of correctional practitioners regarding the severity of intermediate sanctions. Nevertheless, the literature does give some insight.

Role orientation perceptions seem to be the most relevant part of the existing literature for the topic of this study. The finding that probation and parole officers have conflicting views of their roles (e.g., as either law enforcement officers or social workers) may give some insight into how they view the sanction continuum. Numerous studies indicate that many officers used a combination of the two roles to perform their jobs (see Fulton, Stichman, Travis, & Latessa, 1997 and Studt, 1978, for examples).

Hardyman (1988) found that some officers rotate between the two roles, depending on the perceived character and behavior of the offender. Consequently, the role adopted can influence not only the way a practitioner conducts his/her daily duties (Clear & O'Leary, 1983), but also her/his belief about the severity of the sanction being supervised. Clear and O'Leary suggest that the amount of probation conditions set by an officer were dependent on attitudes of authority and assistance held by the officer. In other words, officers with more control-oriented philosophies are more likely to enforce a higher number of conditions on a consistent basis. Clear and Latessa (1993), however, suggest that officer attitudes may be secondary to organizational philosophy when it comes to attitudes toward rehabilitation among supervised offenders.

Goals of the correctional organization also play an important role in the perceptions of correctional officials toward intermediate sanctions. Vaughn (1993) found that directors of state correctional institutions felt that citizens view incapacitation as the main goal of correctional facilities and were disinclined toward rehabilitation, in relation to other goals. Furthermore, the state directors themselves perceived the main goal of their facilities to be deterrence, followed by rehabilitation, incapacitation, and finally retribution. Vaughn noted that the conflict between what directors think the public perceives as goals, and what the public actually perceives as goals, may be problematic for policy implementation.

In a study of correctional facilities in Bermuda Burton, Ju, Dunaway, and Wolfe (1991) determined that offender rehabilitation was the most important goal among correctional officers. Among the officers surveyed, 78% of them believed that rehabilitation was just as important as punishing the offender, while 45% thought that rehabilitation was an effective means of reducing recidivism. As Burton et al. determined that 83% of the surveyed officers rated punishment as the worst way to reduce crime, Bermuda officers seemed to perceive punishment and rehabilitations as direct opposites. Beliefs like these would almost surely help condition the attitudes of correctional officials toward intermediate sanctions.

Despite the previous studies that examine attitudes toward and use of alternative sanctions among judges and correctional officials, no studies of which we are aware have examined the perceptions of these two groups regarding the relative severity of alternative sanctions when compared to prison. Because judges have direct input in decisions about what punishments offenders receive, and correctional officials play a key role in the actual enforcement of the community sanctions that offenders receive, their perceptions of the severity of punishments and, ultimately, the punishment continuum are important. Examining these perceptions can not only expand the body of work surrounding the perceptions of alternative sanctions, but also provide evidence that could lead to more accurate sentences resulting in offenders experiencing the consequences intended by our judicial and correctional systems.

# Public Perceptions of Sanction Severity

Because public opinion impacts so many decisions made by those who enact laws regarding sentencing of offenders and, to a lesser extent, the judges who apply those laws, we feel that it is essential to examine exchange rates among the public as well. In this section, we examine public opinion regarding the relative severity of prison and its historical foundations and compare exchange rates among the public with those of offenders, officers, and judges to examine how the public rates these sanctions in comparison to other groups. We then close the chapter by discussing the importance of attitudes regarding the relative severity of prison when compared to community sanctions for correctional policy.

Despite the voluminous research about public opinion on so many topics (e.g., the death penalty, abortion, gun control), there is limited literature regarding public perceptions of alternative sanctions. Among those studies that have examined this topic, however, there is some evidence to suggest that labeling the public as supporters of "get tough" policies may be problematic. Roberts and Stalans (1997) reviewed several studies and cited research contradicting the viewpoint that the public is excessively punitive. English, Crouch, and Pullen (1989) and Applegate, Cullen, and Fisher (2002) demonstrated that the public was more supportive than judges of utilizing community corrections alternatives for offenders who had not committed serious offenses and who had limited criminal histories. This finding was replicated by data from: responses to a national opinion survey (Haghighi & Lopez, 1998), Minnesota residents (Bae, 1991), Missouri residents (Fichter & Veneziano, 1988), and jurors (Diamond & Stalans. 1989). Roberts and Stalans also determined from public opinion surveys of Michigan residents that two out of three respondents believed that, for offenders with limited criminal histories and who had not committed serious offenses, community-based alternative sanctions should be used instead of prison. Furthermore, given the choice of probation, prison, fines, and fine plus probation for first time burglary offenders, Roberts and Doob (1989) reported that only about one out of three Canadian respondents chose prison over the other sentences. Additionally, half of those who chose prison stated that even though they selected prison for the scenario at hand, they favored community restitution in all or most cases. Finally, Brown and Elrod (1995) found that, under certain conditions, New York residents supported the use of electronic monitoring as an alternative to incarceration.

Research by John Doble Research Associates, Inc. (1995) found that the public preferred the use of alternative sanctions over prison for nonviolent offenders in North Carolina. More than 80% of the respondents agreed that day reporting, house arrest, community service, boot camps, and halfway houses should be used instead of prison for those offenders not convicted of a violent offense. Furthermore, studies by both McCorkle (1993) and Cullen, Skovron, Scott, and Burton (1990) suggest that members of the public generally support rehabilitative programs for inmates that afford them better opportunities for success upon release from prison. Thus, the punitiveness of the public (as viewed through the eyes of policymakers) appears to be exaggerated.

The research reviewed above reveals that, among members of the lay public, alternative sanctions are often preferred over prison. Nevertheless, none of the studies reviewed above dealt explicitly with exchange rates, or preferences in the *amount* of an alternative sanction that respondents would choose given a choice between that alternative and prison. In this chapter, we begin the effort to fill that gap.

# Results

## Judges' Sample

As described in Chapter 2, responses from the sample of 71 judges used here were collected via surveys during the fall of 2004 from all the county judges that were currently serving in the state of Kentucky and had presided over a circuit court (or were currently in that role). Data from 208 officers who supervised clients in the state of Kentucky that were collected in January and February 2004 are also used here. Demographics for both these groups appear in Table 6.1.

Results presented in Table 6.1 indicate that, while the judges (Mean age = 53.8 years) were generally older than the officers (Mean age = 39.6 years), both groups were largely male (60.1% of the officers and 84.3% of the judges) and White (93.8% of the officers and 97.1% of the judges). The vast majority of both groups were college graduates, while an additional 25.5 % of the officers and almost all of the judges had taken some postgraduate classes or completed law school. Two officers (1 percent) responded that they had taken some college classes; these officers were likely "grandfathered" for the college education requirement that now applies to officers in Kentucky.

Table 6.1  Descriptive Statistics for Officers and Judges

|  | Officers | Judges |
|---|---|---|
| Mean Age | 39.6 | 53.8 |
| Gender<br>  Male<br>  Female | <br>125 (60.1%)<br>82 (39.4%) | <br>60(84.3%)<br>11(15.7%) |
| Ethnicity<br>  White<br>  Black | <br>195 (93.8%)<br>11 (5.3%) | <br>69(97.1%)<br>2 (2.9%) |
| Highest level of Education Completed<br>  Some College<br>  College Graduate<br>  Some Graduate/Professional studies | <br>2(1.0%)<br>151(72.6%)<br>53(25.5%) | <br>1(1.4%)<br>2 (2.8%)<br>68(95.8%) |

## Public Sample

The original data for this study were collected from a sample of 1,313 Kentucky residents; the data collection process was described earlier in Chapter 2. Given the racial differences in exchange rates among offenders, we excluded all respondents that did not identify themselves as either White or Black. As such, the sample under study here consists of 1,273 respondents.

Of the 1273 general public respondents who provided data for this study, the results presented in Table 6.2 indicate that slightly over half (55.4%) were male and almost all (91.2%) were White. One in five respondents (19.8%) was a college graduate, while an additional 7.1% had taken some postgraduate classes. Almost half (44.1%) of the respondents had graduated high school although 1 in 10 (10.0%) had not completed high school. Respondents were evenly distributed across most age groups, with almost half the respondents (42.6%) indicating that they were between 25 and 45 years of age. Respondents were also fairly evenly distributed across income categories, although one in five respondents (20.6%) had an annual income of over $75,000.

## Judges, the Public, and Corrections Officials

Given that 1) no research compares exchange rates of judges and/or probation and parole officers with those of any other group and 2) we had access to data regarding exchange rates from offenders (probationers and parolees) in Kentucky from the study reported in the previous chapters, we were able to

Table 6.2  Characteristics of the Sample of Kentucky Residents

| Demographic Variable | Sample (Frequency & %) |
|---|---|
| Gender | |
| Male | 727 (55.4) |
| Female | 580 (44.2) |
| Missing Data | 6 (.5) |
| Race | |
| White | 1197 (91.2) |
| Black | 76 (5.8) |
| Other | 35 (2.7) |
| Missing Data | 5 (.4) |
| Marital Status | |
| Married | 934 (71.1) |
| Unmarried | 364 (27.7) |
| Missing Data | 15 (1.1) |
| Age | |
| 18–24 | 201 (9.6) |
| 25–35 | 434 (20.6) |
| 36–45 | 458 (22.0) |
| 46–55 | 383 (18.4) |
| 56–65 | 282 (13.6) |
| 66 and over | 207 (9.5) |
| Missing Data | 126 (6.0) |
| Education | |
| No high school diploma | 126 (10.0) |
| High school Diploma or GED | 562 (44.1) |
| Some College | 210 (16.6) |
| College Graduate | 253 (19.8) |
| Some Graduate or Professional | 89 (7.1) |
| Missing Data | 73 (5.6) |
| Income | |
| Less than $10,000 | 110 (8.4) |
| $10,001–$20,000 | 181 (13.8) |
| $20,001–$30,000 | 119 (9.1) |
| $30,001–$40,000 | 174 (13.3) |
| $40,001–$50,000 | 149 (11.4) |
| $50,001–$75,000 | 198 (15.2) |
| Over $75,000 | 269 (20.6) |
| Missing Data | 106 (8.1) |

compare the mean exchange rates of Kentucky residents alongside Kentucky judges and officers with those of offenders under community supervision. These comparisons are presented in Table 6.3.

The results presented in Table 6.3 reflect the following important findings. First, and most importantly, none of the groups viewed prison as the most severe sanction. Each of the four groups believed that both boot camp and jail are far more punitive than prison, although offenders believed that county jail was significantly more punitive than any of the non-offender groups. With the exception of the general public responses (where the general public agreed to serve significantly more time than the offenders), the exchange rates for boot camp appear remarkably consistent, as there was less than one day's difference between the means for offenders, officers, and judges (6.05 to 6.19 months).

Second, with the exception of the public respondents, the results for each group also suggest that each group viewed at least one alternative sanction served in the community (day fine) to be almost equivalent to prison in terms of punitiveness. Third, the exchange rates offered by offenders were concentrated in a much narrower range of duration than those generated by judges, officers, and the general public. Exchange rates varied from 5.54 months to 23.56 months for offenders. For judges the range was from 6.19 to 39.59, for officers it was 6.05 to 44.23 months, and for the general public respondents, the range was 6.85 to 26.52 months. Fourth, the results presented in Table 6.3 suggest that offenders routinely rate alternatives as more punitive than do judges, officers, and the general public—with the exception of community service, where offenders would serve over twice as much time in community service as officers, and almost 400 more hours to avoid 12 months in prison than would judges . For every other sanction, however, the exchange rates for offenders were lower than those for either the public, the judges, or the officers—meaning that offenders would serve less of a given alternative to avoid 12 months of imprisonment and viewed alternatives as more severe than do judges or officers. Finally, the least severe sanction in all four groups was regular probation; nevertheless, offenders clearly viewed probation as much more punitive than any of the other three groups as judges, officers, and the public would serve nearly twice the amount of probation to avoid imprisonment as would offenders. Relatedly, offenders appeared more willing to serve time in prison than the other three groups when compared to alternatives. Note that the least severe sanction in all four groups was regular probation, which supports the contention of Morris and Tonry that probation is likely the least severe of correctional sanctions.

For each sanction, there were a number of offenders and a small number of officers who stated that they would not do *any amount* of the sanction in question to avoid 12 months in prison. In reference to offenders, 1 in 20 officers (4.9%) felt that convicted offenders would refuse to do any amount of day fine, and 1 in 25 (3.9%) felt that convicted offenders would not participate in any amount of boot camp. For all the other sanctions, less than 1 in 50 officers

Table 6.3  Comparison of Mean Exchange Rates among Offenders, Judges, Officers, and the Public*

| Alt. Sanction | Offenders (1) | | | Judges (2) | | | Officers (3) | | | Public (4) | | |
|---|---|---|---|---|---|---|---|---|---|---|---|---|
| | N | Mean | St.D. | N | Mean | St.D. | N | Mean | St.D. | N | Mean | St.D. |
| County Jail | 587 | 5.54[2,3,4] | 4.81 | 65 | 7.38[1] | 3.71 | 206 | 8.12[1] | 5.79 | 1191 | 8.36[1] | 5.76 |
| Boot Camp | 574 | 6.07[4] | 5.54 | 67 | 6.19 | 3.72 | 206 | 6.05 | 4.02 | 1174 | 6.85[1] | 5.96 |
| Electronic Monitoring | 584 | 13.95[3,4] | 11.82 | 68 | 16.25 | 7.94 | 206 | 17.57[1] | 12.15 | 1199 | 16.02[1] | 13.18 |
| Probation | 584 | 23.56[2,3,4] | 16.54 | 66 | 39.59[1,4] | 24.95 | 206 | 44.23[1,4] | 25.61 | 1185 | 26.52[1,2,3] | 21.82 |
| Comm. Service** | 583 | 1817.29[3] | 1747.34 | 62 | 1440.00[3] | 2145.44 | 199 | 700.50[1,2] | 1013.82 | – | – | – |
| Day Reporting | 582 | 17.01[2,3,4] | 14.96 | 63 | 32.83[1,3,4] | 25.21 | 206 | 22.62[1,2] | 20.24 | 1179 | 21.08[1,2] | 18.34 |
| Int. Incarceration | 585 | 14.60[4] | 12.34 | 62 | 17.58 | 10.60 | 206 | 16.88 | 13.21 | 1185 | 16.75[1] | 12.67 |
| Halfway House | 583 | 14.42[2,4] | 11.96 | 64 | 18.47[1] | 12.96 | 206 | 15.62 | 10.48 | 1185 | 16.15[1] | 11.17 |
| Day Fines | 573 | 12.22[2,4] | 12.80 | 57 | 15.62[1,3] | 24.39 | 205 | 13.48[2] | 18.83 | 1159 | 16.90[1] | 20.70 |

[1] Signifies that this group is significantly different (p<.05) than Group 1 (ANOVA)
[2] Signifies that this group is significantly different (p<.05) than Group 2 (ANOVA)
[3] Signifies that this group is significantly different (p<.05) than Group 3 (ANOVA)
[4] Signifies that this group is significantly different (p<.05) than Group 4 (ANOVA)
* For comparisons of groups with equal variance (electronic monitoring, intermediate incarceration, and halfway house), the Bonferroni test was used to determine significance of differences between groups (because it controls for multiple comparisons between groups). For group comparisons with unequal variance (county jail, boot camp, probation, community service, day reporting, and day fines), the Games-Howell test was used to determine significance of differences between groups.
** A question to assess the exchange rate for community service was not included in the instrument from which the public data were gathered. As such, no data regarding the punitiveness of community service were available for the public respondents.

felt that convicted offenders would refuse to engage in that sanction to avoid 12 months in prison. Additionally, two judges (2.8%) were unwilling to serve any time in county jail to avoid 12 months in prison and one judge was unwilling to serve any time on boot camp to avoid that same sentence. For each of the other sanctions, all of the judges were willing to serve at least some time on that sanction to avoid 12 months in prison.

Offenders, however, had very different responses regarding whether they would refuse to serve any amount of an alternative to avoid 12 months prison. In fact, one in five offenders (19.2%) stated that they would refuse to serve any amount of boot camp to avoid 12 months in prison, with day fines (17.6%) and county jail (17.4%) having almost as high a percentage of refusals. It appears, then, that for a significant core of offenders, prison was preferred over any duration of an alternative.

In Table 6.4, we used the exchange rate means in Table 6.3 to generate a crude ranking of sanction severity for each of the four groups. Prison is given a score of 12.00 (months) because all other sanctions are in reference to one year of imprisonment. The comparisons reveal that each group believed probation was the least punitive sanction while day reporting was also viewed as a relatively lenient punishment by all four groups (ranking just above probation in terms of punitiveness for all three non-offender groups). Additionally, offenders viewed community service (where they were willing to serve approximately 22 months to avoid 12 months in prison) as far less punitive than judges or officers. Surprisingly, officers ranked community service as even more severe than imprisonment (3rd in the severity ranking compared to 7th among judges and 9th among offenders). Quite possibly, judges (and officers) may rank community service as more severe due to concerns about shame and embarrassment they would experience while performing their service in the community; offenders likely experienced less concern with regard to such reputational damage.

With the exception of the general public sample, each group also viewed day fine as relatively punitive, ranking it just behind prison in terms of punitiveness. It seems likely that the general public was not particularly knowledgeable about day fine or its restrictive nature, despite the description provided in the survey. Each of the four groups viewed halfway house and intermittent incarceration as less punitive than prison, with both falling somewhere in the middle of the severity ranking for each group. Finally, officers ranked electronic monitoring much lower in the severity ranking (8th) than did offenders, judges, and the public (each of whom ranked electronic monitoring 4th or 5th). Officers clearly viewed community service as punitive, but viewed electronic monitoring as less severe than any of the remaining three groups.

Table 6.4  Comparison of Sanction Severity Rankings Among
Offenders, Judges, Officers, and the Public Based on
Mean Exchange Rates in Table 6.3*

| Severity Ranking | Offenders | Judges | Officers | Public |
|---|---|---|---|---|
| Most Severe | County Jail | Boot Camp | Boot Camp | Boot Camp |
| | Boot Camp | County Jail | County Jail | County Jail |
| | Prison | Prison | Community Service | Prison |
| | Day Fines | Day Fines | Prison | NA** |
| | Electronic Monitoring | Electronic Monitoring | Day Fines | Electronic Monitoring |
| | Halfway House | Intermittent Incarceration | Halfway House | Halfway House |
| | Intermittent Incarceration | Community Service | Intermittent Incarceration | Intermittent Incarceration |
| | Day Reporting | Halfway House | Electronic Monitoring | Day Fines |
| | Community Service | Day Reporting | Day Reporting | Day Reporting |
| Least Severe | Regular Probation | Regular Probation | Regular Probation | Regular Probation |

* With regard to community service, we assigned respondents 20 hours per week, at four weeks per month based on the total hours of community service for each group in Table 6.2. Few offenders perform that much community service per week and our calculation of months of community service may serve to inflate the punitiveness of community service.
** A question to assess the exchange rate for community service was not included in the instrument from which the public data were gathered. As such, no data regarding the punitiveness of community service were available for the public respondents.

# Discussion

In this chapter, we combined data collected from Kentucky residents, judges, and probation and parole officers with data from Kentucky probationers and parolees to compare exchange rates of criminal justice practitioners with those of probationers and parolees and the general public. Results suggest that, with limited exceptions, exchange rates offered by the public more closely resembled exchange rates provided by the practitioner samples than those of the offenders. With the exception of community service, judges would serve longer amounts of alternative sanctions to avoid prison than would offenders. Furthermore, for county jail, regular probation, day reporting, halfway house, and day fines, there were statistically significant differences in the exchange rates among the two groups. In each of these cases, the exchange rates of the judges were *higher* than those of offenders, indicating that judges felt prison was a more stringent sanction (when compared to these alternative sanctions) than did offenders.

Officers were more willing than offenders to engage in community sanctions as well; with the exception of boot camp (where the ratings were practically identical) and community service (where officers were willing to do far less time on community service), officers were willing to serve more time in the community to avoid prison than offenders, and for jail, electronic monitoring, probation, and day reporting, these differences were statistically significant. Additionally, although the Kentucky residents provided exchange rates closer to the offenders' exchange rates than either judges or probation and parole officers for several of the sanctions, Kentucky residents were significantly more willing than offenders to engage in each community sanction.

Nevertheless, the findings reported here also reveal that judges, while offering higher exchange rates than offenders, differ slightly from officers and the general public in their exchange rates as well. Judges offered significantly lower exchange rates than probation and parole officers for community service and significantly higher exchange rates than officers for day reporting and day fines. Judges offered significantly higher exchange rates than the public for probation and day reporting as well. Additionally, though the differences were not statistically significant, judges would serve less probation and electronic monitoring and more intermittent incarceration and halfway house than the officers to avoid prison. Interestingly, the mean exchange rates for jail were almost identical among each of the four groups.

The results from this research suggest six important conclusions with implications for policy. First, none of the groups surveyed (Kentucky residents, judges, officers, nor offenders) view prison as the harshest punishment. In fact, if there is one universal finding across the four groups, it is that 12 months in medium-security prison is roughly equivalent to between six and eight months in boot camp or jail. We have now replicated this finding in three states (Oklahoma, Indiana, and Kentucky) among five types of respondents (judges, probation/parole officers, probationers/parolees, prisoners, and the general public). As such, the general public and the clients and practitioners in the criminal justice system agree that boot camp and jail (no matter where that camp or jail is located) is approximately twice as punitive as medium security prison.

Second, in comparison to offenders and judges (these data were not available for the general public), officers would serve far less time in community service to avoid prison. Judges and offenders evidently feel that community service is less hassle than do officers. Officers appear to view community service as a far more punitive sanction than the judges responsible for sentencing offenders to community service and the offenders sentenced to community service. It could be that this discrepancy is due to the familiarity that officers have with the delivery of community service, and that officers interpret community service as more onerous than either offenders or judges. And depending on their role orientation (Gordon et al., 2003; Kifer et al., 2003), officers may be either more likely (punitive role orientation) or less likely (social worker orientation) to recommend community service as a condition of an offender's community sanction. Those officers who manifest a punitive role orientation may use community service as a "club" to either force offenders into compliance with community supervision or design conditions to make it easier to violate offenders, based on knowledge that they will be unlikely to complete the sanction given the onerous nature (from the officer's perspective) of community service. Officers with a social work orientation, on the other hand, may be less likely to use community service as one of the conditions of probation or parole based on their sentiment that offenders will not comply with the requirements of community service and will be less likely to complete the sentence. Irrespective of role orientation, it is apparent that the officers view community service as more onerous than the offenders sentenced to community service, and this difference may have dramatic implications for community service as a condition of probation or parole.

A third policy implication of this finding is that when community/local sanctions (electronic monitoring, halfway house, day reporting, and day fines) are compared with imprisonment, judges feel these sanctions are far less punitive than the offenders sentenced to those sanctions. This has major implications for sentencing strategies that are often based on the assumption that revocation followed by imprisonment represents a "ratcheting up" of sanction severity as a means of enforcing compliance with conditions. The present findings may contradict that assumption and suggest that, for many offenders, the "hammer" of incarceration for technical violations of community supervision is not perceived as a significant increase (or any increase at all) in sanction severity. Indeed, the findings presented here suggest that judges would do as well, or perhaps better, to rely on threats of electronic monitoring, day reporting, day fine, boot camp, or jail to enforce compliance. Our findings suggest that revocation and subsequent imprisonment is not as punitive to offenders as officers or judges may wish them to be, and supervision strategies that take this into account might assist in reducing the extent to which probation/parole revocations presently contribute to prison crowding.

Fourth, in results presented elsewhere, Moore et al. (2007) determined that exchange rates for day reporting, halfway house, and day fine were best explained in a context whereby a number of factors combine to influence decision-making processes among the judges under study here. When considering the restrictions associated with these sanctions, all are fairly restrictive but still allow a participant to be somewhat bonded to society. Judges may be acutely aware that sentences are most effective when offenders can maintain contacts and support systems with the community or family while serving out sentences. This assumption may also explain the higher exchange rates offered by judges for day fines, day reporting, and, to a lesser extent, halfway house when compared to offenders, officers, and the public. These particular sanctions may appeal to judges in that they might offer "restrictive flexibility" that can satisfy the public outcry for punishment while also allowing individuals to maintain bonds they have with family or community. This initial attraction may bring about a more positive overall view of such sanctions, which, inevitably, converts into higher exchange rates.

Fifth, though the initial tendency might be to simply dichotomize the four populations explored herein (i.e., offenders, officers, the public, and judges) into either offending or non-offending groups, it is important that the public, judges, and officers be viewed as separate groups due to the tendencies revealed in the data comparison. Like offenders, judges were found to have significantly different mean exchange rates than officers for three alternative sanctions (community service, day reporting, and day fines). Interestingly, in each case, judicial exchange rates were higher than those offered by the probation and parole officers. As such, the data collected here would primarily suggest that, of the three groups explored, judges find prison the most punitive. An alternative explanation is that judges may underestimate the punitive nature of alternative sanctions. This underestimation would be less likely to occur in either the offender or officer population due to their direct experience of either undergoing or enforcing each sanction. However, when comparing all four populations, the data suggest that more direct experience with the justice system tends to be associated with less willingness to serve alternatives to avoid imprisonment.

Finally, offenders were far more likely to refuse to do any amount of an alternative sanction than judges or officers. Some offenders feel that any agreement to participate in alternative sanctions only prolongs the inevitability of recidivism and incarceration. In other words, they feel the likelihood of being revoked and incarcerated is so high that they prefer to go to prison immediately, rather than attempt to meet the requirements of an alternative sanction and end up in prison anyway following revocation. As mentioned earlier, this finding calls into question the idea that the revocation-imprisonment sequence, which assumes that imprisonment is the most punitive sanction, and that the threat of imprisonment is a means of enforcing compliance with conditions, will work to insure compliance with community sanctions. Our work contradicts that assumption and suggests that supervision and sentencing strategies based on this logic may be misdirected.

At a more fundamental level, the basic options currently used for encouraging compliance with probation/parole conditions are to: a) reward or give incentives for compliant behavior or b) punish, or threaten to punish, non-compliance. In general, community supervision strategies have placed far more emphasis on the latter than the former. Yet the effectiveness of the latter approach is in no small way contingent on the assumption that offenders, judges, and officers share similar subjective definitions of the level of punishment associated with various sanctions. Our findings challenge this assumption and, hence, the viability of supervision strategies based on the assumption.

It also appears that officers and judges feel that most (if not all) offenders can successfully complete alternative sanctions if they so desire. While this disjunction in opinion may be expected given the diametrically opposed roles in the criminal justice system, it is enlightening as well. Officers' and judges' confidence that offenders can complete alternative sanctions is likely a function of the "success stories" that they have encountered in their careers. As the findings in Tables 6.3 and 6.4 reveal, offenders rate probation as significantly more punitive than do officers or judges. Thus, regardless of the explanation for this finding, offenders, judges, and officers have divergent views on the nature (and perhaps severity) of regular probation as an alternative to prison.

To lessen the divide between practitioner and offender expectations, it might be helpful for probation/parole agencies to establish a "mentoring program" for new offenders under their supervision, with past "success stories" used as the mentors. To expose an offender who is serving an alternative sanction for the first time to a mentor who has successfully completed that same sanction could be helpful in a number of ways. First, it would give the newly sentenced offender a positive role model, a person similar to them who successfully completed the alternative sanction in question. Second, it would let the newly sentenced offender know that successful completion of the sentence is possible even though they may consider completion unlikely, and they may begin to develop confidence that they too can successfully complete the alternative sanction.

The findings presented in this chapter are not without limitations. There was little variation by gender or race in the judge and officer sample, two of the strongest predictors of preference for prison over alternative sanctions among offenders. As such, research examining practitioner perspectives should be conducted with larger, more diverse samples from other regions to insure that the findings presented here are not an artifact of the sample used. In addition, research regarding the relative severity of correctional sanctions should be extended to legislators and other criminal justice officials to determine how their exchange rates compare with those groups under study here. To develop a range of sanctions that is more effective at controlling recidivism and more just in delivering punishments input from all the aforementioned groups should be considered.

Within the limitations of our data, however, results presented here allow for the exploration of the perceptions of the "continuum of punishment" among judges, offenders, officers, and the general public. Judges and officers play an integral role in the sentencing and supervision processes, and a better understanding of their perceptions of the punishments they impose and deliver should inform the development and implementation of a system of community-based sanctions that more accurately embodies principles of desert and proportionate punishment in our criminal justice system.

# CHAPTER 7

# ARE CORRECTIONAL SANCTIONS CRIMINOGENIC?

## Testing for a Positive Punishment Effect among Incarcerated Offenders

America's increased reliance upon prisons and community-based sanctions to "solve" the crime problem are often cited in the literature (Garland, 2001; Lotzke & Ziedenburg, 2005; Mauer, 2001). The sheer number of individuals incarcerated in American prisons and jails is staggering with recent estimates approaching 2.4 million incarcerated in December 2008, and another 5.1 million serving non-custodial sanctions (PEW, 2009). America accounts for one quarter of the world's prisoners and boasts the highest incarceration rate in the world with 762 inmates per 100,000 U.S. residents in December 2007—a 700% increase in the last 30 years (Pastore and McGuire, 2008). Between 1970 and 2000, America added over 2 million inmates, and correctional populations are expected to increase into the foreseeable future (King, Mauer, & Young, 2005). Currently, 1 in every 100 adults in America is incarcerated, and 1 in every 31 is under some form of correctional control—in state or federal prisons, in jails, or under some form of community supervision.

With greater dependence upon punishment comes an increased responsibility to evaluate the effects of punishment experiences. Any research suggesting that those who experience correctional punishments are more likely to commit crime than those not punished—or those punished to a lesser degree—is of particular interest. Lawrence Sherman notes, "If our first duty is to do no harm, then criminology is morally compelled to identify the ways in which punishment may be causing crime and to invent alternatives to criminogenic practices" (1993, p. 446). Given the number of individuals released from prison each year or serving community-based sanctions, any process that increases the likelihood of re-offending among this population should be subject to intense empirical scrutiny.

To be sure, there are a number of conceivable reasons individuals who have been punished more than others might be more inclined to commit crime. First, many scholars and laypersons are convinced that the experience of close

24/7 interaction with other offenders over an extended period has an independent criminogenic effect through a process of experiential learning in the prison environment. Further, the experience of being punished activates an entire state apparatus of social control and surveillance. Probation officers, parole officers, police, and informal agents of social control are aware of one's status as a prior offender and will subsequently monitor and survey one's actions on a more regular basis. Consequently, offenders on community supervision are more likely to be rearrested even if actual rates of offending behavior remain constant. Further, reentry into the community is often difficult and stressful, with reduced options for housing, employment, and income that may encourage re-offending, as well as the stigma conferred on ex-convicts. Attempts to explain the effect of correctional sanctions on future offending should acknowledge that these "collateral" or "invisible" punishments (independently or in combination) may cause released offenders to commit more crimes. Complicating matters is that released offenders often return to the same communities, circumstances, and acquaintances that encouraged their initial criminal behaviors. To disentangle these many likely contributors to re-offending is a complex task well beyond the scope of the present effort, but it seems important that we attempt to examine their relative impacts on habitual offending.

Having experienced what is commonly perceived as the most severe correctional sanction our system regularly imposes (imprisonment), over 700,000 offenders are now being released from the nation's prisons and jails each year to join the ranks of the over 5 million offenders who currently serve non-custodial sanctions. The manner in which correctional punishments alter the world-views, opinions, attitudes, and behaviors of those who have been punished is of central interest to criminologists and correctional practitioners. Particularly relevant is a) how the experience of criminal justice sanctions shapes the perceptions of costs and benefits that presumably motivate re-offending, and b) how imprisonment impacts offenders' likelihood of re-offending upon release. These two interrelated linkages address the issue of specific deterrence among those who have been punished. As noted in prior work (Nagin, 1998; Paternoster, 1987; Pogarsky, Piquero, & Paternoster, 2004), the first linkage involves a perceptual process in which correctional sanctions and other experiences impact perceptions about the certainty and severity of punishment. The second linkage involves a behavioral process in which perceptions of certainty and severity of punishment as well as prior punishment experiences impact subsequent offending behaviors. The bulk of research on deterrence and rational choice has focused almost exclusively on the second of these linkages: the manner in which sanction experiences and risk perceptions influence decisions to re-offend (Nagin, 1998; Pogarsky, Piquero, & Paternoster, 2004).

Meanwhile, only a relatively small body of work has focused on the first linkage. For both issues (i.e., the development of risk perceptions and how these perceptions influence offending), the available research relies heavily on non-offending student and general population samples and studies of relatively less serious law-breaking (i.e., drinking, drunk driving, pot smoking, truancy) and/or presents respondents with hypothetical scenarios that they react to (hypothetically) by selecting from a set of behavioral options provided to them by the researcher (Carmichael et al., 2005; Paternoster & Piquero, 1995; Piquero & Pogarsky, 2002; Pogarsky & Piquero, 2003; Wright et al., 2004).

While these methodological conventions are well established in the research literature and are generally accepted by deterrence scholars, it is likely that perceived costs and benefits of offending differ depending on the population under study, and the views of convicted offenders who have experienced correctional sanctions are critically important when examining decision-making processes associated with criminal behavior, particularly since it has been argued that sanction threat perceptions are influenced by information gained from prior experience with offending and consequences associated with that offending (Stafford & Warr, 1993; Pogarsky et al., 2004). The focus on adult criminal offenders is a unique feature of the work presented in this chapter, where we use a sample of over 700 incarcerated adult offenders serving time in a large southern correctional center to explore the impact of correctional punishment experiences on offenders perceptions of the certainty of future sanctions and self-reported likelihood to re-offend after release.

# Deterrence versus the Positive Punishment Effect

Deterrence doctrine predicts that punishment experiences should reduce the likelihood of offending (Bentham, 1998; Gibbons, 1992). This statement is not only central to our "commonsense" understandings of crime and punishment but it is also the foundation of modern criminal justice policy. Nevertheless, empirical evidence supporting deterrence is equivocal at best (Pratt, Cullen, Blevins, Daigle, & Madensen; 2006). Meta-analyses and narrative reviews of the literature present mixed empirical support for deterrence theory (Nagin, 1998; Pratt et al., 2006; Paternoster, 1987). Paternoster's review of empirical work investigating the effect of perceived certainty and severity of punishment on future criminal activity between 1972 and 1986 concluded that studies variously find a moderately large inverse relationship, a weak inverse relationship, a positive relationship, and no relationship between perceived certainty of punishment and criminal behavior. Although many of the studies Paternoster reviewed found an inverse relationship—albeit a weak one—he suggests the causal order between perceptions of certainty of punishment on subsequent criminal behavior could reasonably be reversed to represent an "experiential effect." The experiential effect suggests that individuals adjust their perceptions of likelihood of punishment after they commit crimes and go undetected (or punished). Because most studies are cross-sectional surveys and only incorporate measures at one time, temporal ordering of variables is difficult to establish. Paternoster also raises an even more fundamental concern regarding claims of deterrence.

> Perceptual deterrence researchers and proponents of the deterrence doctrine should also begin to prepare themselves for possible bad news. No matter how sophisticated the study or how valiant the effort, very little relationship may exist between people's estimates of the certainty of and severity of punishment and their behavior. Deterrence theory assumes that even if people do not perceive accurately the objective certainty and severity of punishment, at least they are motivated rationally by their perceptions of those risks. Perhaps not; it may not be in the nature of the beast to be so rational ... We are probably minimally rational (Paternoster, 1987, p. 214).

More recently, evidence from state panel data finds that the increase in offenders released from prison is significantly associated with increases in crime rates (Vieraitis, Kovandzic, & Marvell, 2007). Vieriatis and colleagues attribute observed increases in crime rates that follow prison releases to the criminogenic effects of prison. Though their study—which uses state-level data—cannot explicate the specific pathways that lead individuals from release to recidivism, they are convinced that, for many offenders, incarceration increases the likelihood of crime after release. Similarly, Nieuwbeerta, Nagin and Blokland (unpublished manuscript) use data from the Netherlands-Based Criminal Career and Life-Course Study and find that first-time imprisonment is associated with an increase in criminal activity in the three years following release. Nieuwbeerta et al. propose that their findings reflect a criminogenic effect of the experience of imprisonment, but like Vieriatis they can only speculate on the specific factors that generate such an outcome and recommend that future research focus on potential mechanisms that might cause a criminogenic effect. They note that the lack of evidence regarding the effects of imprisonment is surprising, particularly because incarceration is such a common sanction for serious crime in the Western World (Nieuwbeerta et al., unpublished manuscript).

Daniel Nagin (1998) provides a more optimistic assessment of the deterrent effect of the criminal justice system when he argues that evidence is much

stronger than originally believed. Nagin categorizes deterrence research conducted since 1980 into the following three categories: 1) interrupted time-se-
ries, 2) ecological, and 3) perceptual studies. According to Nagin, "With few
exceptions, the perceptual studies find that self-reported criminality is lower
among people who perceive that sanction risks and cost are higher" (Nagin,
1998, p. 52). For Nagin, these perceptual studies are the most recent evidence
that strengthens the claims of deterrence theorists despite the fact that they
rely on data from primarily non-offending samples. Although the empirical
evidence cited by Nagin does support deterrence theory, it is only one linkage.
The other linkage between sanctions and perceptions of risks has been largely
neglected (Pogarsky et al., 2004).

Contrary to the predictions of deterrence theory, which claims that the experience of being punished will reduce future offending, recent work has suggested the existence of a "positive punishment" or "emboldening" effect whereby
the experience of being punished increases the likelihood of future criminal
behavior (Paternoster & Piquero, 1995; Piquero & Pogarsky, 2002; Piquero &
Paternoster, 1998 Pogarsky & Piquero, 2003; Sherman, 1993). Several explanations for this positive punishment effect have been proposed.

Sherman (1993) forwards a theory of "defiance" that he says helps explain
the conditions under which punishment increases subsequent deviance. Sherman argues that punishment that is perceived as unjust, unfair, or excessive
can lead to unacknowledged shame and defiant pride, which in turn increases
future criminal behavior. To our knowledge, this explanation has received only
limited empirical testing, though Bouffard and Piquero (2008) offer a recent
attempt that they argue provides "suggestive evidence in favor of the basic
tenets of defiance theory" (Bouffard & Piquero, 2008, p. 22).

Another explanation for the positive punishment effect involves a selection
bias, where those with more prior punishment experiences are simply the most
committed offenders who will tend to report a greater likelihood of future offending (Piquero & Pogarsky, 2002; Pogarsky & Piquero, 2003). Thus, the
criminal justice system merely acts as a sorting or selection mechanism by
which those most committed offenders are identified. In this case, "punishment experience coincides with but does not encourage further offending"
(Pogarsky & Piquero, 2003, p. 98). No causal claim is made, so the criminal
justice system simply earmarks those with criminogenic tendencies. Nevertheless, this account fails to address why some offenders are more committed
than others, and does not claim that punishment increases the likelihood of future crimes.

A third account of the positive punishment effect claims that offenders engage in a "gambler's fallacy" with regard to the chances of future apprehension.
Under this "resetting" hypothesis, offenders "reset their sanction-certainty es-

timate, apparently believing they would have to be exceedingly unlikely to be apprehended again." (Pogarsky & Piquero, 2003, p. 96). In this case, offenders feel that apprehension is a rare event, and once they've been caught they feel the chances of being apprehended again are unlikely—a miscalculation of the likelihood of apprehension (certainty) that then encourages future offending (Piquero & Paternoster, 1998; Piquero & Pogarsky, 2002; Pogarsky & Piquero, 2003). Criminals may believe that after being caught and punished for a crime the odds of being apprehended and punished again are reduced, and they could not be that "unlucky" again the next time they offend. This phenomenon can be likened to a gambler who raises the stakes after losing several hands in the belief that he/she is "due for some good luck." The gambler's fallacy has been cited as an explanation for why criminals might reduce their sanction-certainty estimates, which increases their likelihood of re-offending.

## The Gambler's Fallacy

The gambler's fallacy is a term describing the faulty reasoning of individuals who mistakenly believe that the odds of some event occurring are influenced by prior outcomes. This fallacy is common among all types of people when making calculations concerning the odds of some event occurring. Joseph Cowan expresses many of the sentiments illustrative of the gambler's fallacy in the following passage:

> If several heads in a row have come up in flipping a coin, many people will declare tails likely on the next throw. If several blacks successfully have come up at the roulette table, many people will assert the high probability of a red on the next spin ... Sports broadcasters will often announce something like: "McSwish has struck out his last seven times at bat, so he's about due to really tear the cover off the ball (Cowan, 1969, p. 238).

A similar process may operate among criminals whereby perceptions of certainty of punishment are systematically underestimated due to an illusion of control, perhaps through the experience of doing crime successfully without being caught. Certainly most criminals have successfully committed many more crimes than that for which they were apprehended, which would emphasize the improbability of apprehension. Additionally, criminals may be particularly vulnerable to this interpretation due to a tendency to compare their level of control with others in the immediate social context. Because prisons are full of those who have failed to escape detection, there is no shortage of examples of what not to do. Borrowing from what has been termed the self-serving bias; individuals within the context of prisons will tend to view themselves as above average in terms of control over likelihood of being apprehended, even if this is not the case. The self-serving bias involves a dynamic where persons are likely to interpret circumstances, situations, and judgments as more favorable to themselves than to others (Piquero & Pogarsky, 2002; Ross & Sicoly, 1979; Svenson, 1981). Despite prior punishment experiences, offenders may feel they are better at avoiding apprehension than others, perceive a lower certainty of apprehension, and be more motivated to offend. The self-serving bias would then presumably explain a positive punishment effect.

# Recent Work on the Positive Punishment Effect and the Gambler's Fallacy

In their test of Stafford and Warr's (1993) reconceptualization of deterrence, Piquero and Paternoster (1998) proposed the gambler's fallacy to explain a positive association between being detained at a DUI checkpoint, and likelihood to drink and drive in the future. The study analyzed secondary data from a 1986 telephone survey that focused upon licensed drivers over the age of 16. Respondents were asked if they had ever been arrested for driving under the influence, whether they had ever been pulled over at a roadside checkpoint, and how likely they were to be pulled over by the police if they drank six shots of whiskey and drove. The dependent variable, intention to commit crime, was operationalized by the following question: "If I am perfectly honest with myself, I will probably drive at least once in the next year while I am over the legal alcohol limit." Responses to this item were measured using a Likert scales, ranging from strongly disagree to strongly agree. Their results showed that the experience of being pulled over at a roadside checkpoint had a positive relationship with projections to drink and drive, which they cite as an example of a positive punishment effect.

The item used to measure past punishment experience is as follows: "Respondents were asked to estimate the number of times they had ever been pulled over in one of the spot checks where police were stopping cars at random to give drivers a blood alcohol test or a coordination test" (Piquero & Paternoster; 1998). Piquero and Paternoster defend this as a valid measurement of punishment because "being pulled over by a sobriety checkpoint involves elements of anxiety, apprehension, and discomfort that people would choose to avoid, even if the checkpoint results in no further consequence" (Piquero &

Paternoster, 1998, p. 8). The use of this measure as an indicator of prior punishment experience is potentially problematic, however. For example, the number of individuals who experience a sobriety checkpoint and are not arrested is likely greater than those who are arrested, and the measure fails to distinguish between those who are arrested and those who may be drunk but escape detection. If individuals escape detection and arrest, then their perceptions of certainty of arrest would presumably be diminished ("punishment avoidance" as proposed by Stafford and Warr, 1993). In any case, Piquero and Paternoster propose the gambler's fallacy as an explanation for the observed positive association between past punishment experiences and intention to commit crime.

Piquero and Pogarsky (2002) presented a sample of college students with the following scenario:

> Suppose you drove by yourself one evening to meet some friends in a local bar. By the end of the evening, you've had enough drinks so that you are pretty sure your blood alcohol level is above the legal limit. Suppose that you live about ten miles away and you have to be at work early the next morning. You can either drive home or find some other way home, but if you leave your car at the bar, you will have to return early the next morning to pick it up.

Subjects were then asked to estimate the likelihood of being pulled over by the police if they drove home drunk, estimating the level of certainty from 0 to 100. Students were also asked to estimate (on a scale of 0 to 100) the likelihood that they would drive home under the circumstances presented in the scenario (likelihood of offending). The measure of punishment experience asks students to report the number of times they had actually been stopped by police when they believed that their blood alcohol level was above the legal limit. Pogarsky and Piquero (2002) report that "contrary to Stafford and Warr's (1993) reconceptualization and the overall logic of deterrence, however, punishment experiences appear to encourage rather than discourage future offending" (p. 178). They term this dynamic an "emboldening effect" and offer the gambler's fallacy to account for the observed positive punishment association.

Using the same sample of college students and the same scenario of hypothetical drunk driving, Pogarsky and Piquero (2003) proceed to examine the positive punishment effect and the gambler's fallacy more closely. The authors reported finding evidence of the positive punishment effect, with previously punished students being more likely to drive drunk than unpunished students. In addition, they report finding a negative association between their measure of punishment experience (having been pulled over at a DUI stop) and perceived certainty (estimated likelihood of being pulled over by police if driving drunk), which they view as evidence of a gambler's fallacy or resetting effect. After disaggregating the sample into low and high risk groups (based on an index of self-reported past drinking, shoplifting, vandalism, fighting, impulsivity, and delinquency peer influence), Pogarsky and Piquero (2003) report that the gambler's fallacy operates only among "individuals who engage in little offending or related activity" and that "the resetting bias appears to be confined to relatively naïve offenders" (p. 111). Finally, the authors claim to find a greater resetting effect or gambler's fallacy among females because females are disproportionately represented among "naïve" offenders—those in their low-risk category.

# Limitations of Past Research

While the gambler's fallacy is a provocative explanation for crime and its relationship to punishment, and may help explain a positive punishment effect, the few studies that examine these issues are characterized by a number of methodological and measurement problems. First, these studies do not focus upon a sample of primary theoretical interest—criminals. Rather, they routinely employ convenience samples of non-offending populations (i.e., students or the general public). Second, the extant research frequently asks individuals (often students) to imagine themselves in a given scenario they may never have contemplated or experienced, and then to choose among behavioral responses provided by the researchers. It is uncertain how student responses to hypothetical scenarios are relevant to the criminal decision-making and behaviors of adult habitual offenders. Third, researchers often do not measure actual punishment experience, or do not distinguish between fairly routine encounters with police versus actual arrest, or do not account for how actual punishment (arrest and the experience of correctional sanctions) influences perceived certainty. Finally, studies using data from high school or college students frequently focus upon relatively less serious offenses to the exclusion of serious adult drug, property, and violent offenses that draw severe criminal justice consequences.

Given these potential weaknesses in the extant literature, improvement in terms of measurement and the population under study would significantly enhance empirical investigations and generate findings more directly relevant to issues of specific deterrence. Studies of how adult criminal offenders react to correctional sanctions are critical to understanding deterrence, and have clear policy implications. Examination of the gambler's fallacy and the positive punishment effect among adult criminal offenders would seem to provide a unique and interesting extension to this body of research. Furthermore, research might focus upon situations and behaviors that are known to the respondents rather than imagined scenarios. The measurement of past punishment experiences and certainty of future punishment should include arrest and/or actual punishment, not merely surveillance. And research should include serious criminal offenses rather than what might be interpreted as relatively minor offenses.

The measurement of prior punishment would seem to be of critical importance, particularly among a population of offenders who may have a wide range of prior punishment experiences. For example, does having served time in a juvenile facility generate such an effect, or is it limited to adult prisons and jails—or does the experience of both promote offending? Is the positive punishment effect associated with the *amount* of prior imprisonment—regardless of when it may have happened? Is the predicted effect more associated with the duration of punishment the offender is now serving or the amount of the sentence they still must serve? Perhaps the punishment effect is influenced by the *quality* of prior punishment (i.e., how bad was it?). As demonstrated in previous chapters, some offenders who serve time may not view it as particularly punitive. Finally, along with imprisonment, it seems important to examine the potential impact of alternative or community-based sanctions as the vast majority of offenders currently under correctional control (over five million) serve their punishments in the community.

To address some of these questions, we collected data from over 700 incarcerated offenders to examine the association of a range of punishment experience indicators with offenders' perceptions of certainty of arrest if they re-offend, the severity of the sanction (time in prison) they would face if caught, and intentions to re-offend upon release. The work aims to explore the gambler's fallacy and the notion of a positive punishment effect among adult criminal offenders.

# Data and Methods

The data used in this chapter were gathered at a large state correctional center in the South, which held approximately 3,000 inmates at the time of the survey, including all female inmates in the state system (approximately 1,300 at the time). Design of the survey instrument commenced by organizing two focus groups—one with eight male inmates and one with eight female inmates—to solicit their input regarding potential factors that might motivate or inhibit re-offending upon release. Based on prior experience working with inmate populations, current knowledge of the extant literature, and comments from focus group participants, a pilot survey was pre-tested on 21 male and 21 female inmates (separately). Immediately following the pre-test, comments were solicited from pre-test participants in open discussion. The survey was again revised based on pilot survey results and inmate comments. The final self-administered  questionnaire was 11 pages long and required approximately 30 minutes to complete.

Prior to selection of the sample, meetings were held with administrators and wardens from the Department of Corrections (DOC) to determine the best data collection procedure (i.e., the least disruptive method of generating the largest number of respondents). Administrators advised that the optimal procedure would be to have unit managers advertise the data collection effort on the day prior to the arrival of the research team and identify volunteers to participate in the research on the following day.

The final draft of the instrument was administered to samples of male and female inmates in December 2001 and January 2002. The design of the prison was such that there were over 20 housing units of varying security levels dispersed throughout the prison grounds. Inmates were brought to one central meeting space in both the female and male portions of the facility where the study was explained by the research team. Males completed the questionnaire in a large, cafeteria-style room in groups of 50–100 inmates per session in the male portion of the correctional facility; female inmates were surveyed in groups of 20–30 in a smaller conference room on the women's side of the facility during a series of visits to the institution.

For the purposes of this research, inmates were viewed as "experts" who had knowledge about the prison experience and criminal offending that the research team did not. After the research team explained the study, inmates still interested in participating remained seated, while those not wishing to participate were returned to their respective cells. The remaining inmates were then given a more in-depth explanation of the study and a consent form that provided contact information should any participant wish to learn more about the study. Members of the research team remained in the room to answer questions and to ensure that no interaction occurred between respondents and DOC personnel. For security reasons, two or three correctional employees remained in the room at all times, though they stood at one end of the room and tried to be as unobtrusive as possible.

Given the constraints placed upon the research team by the administrators, it is quite possible that there is some type of selection bias due to the voluntary nature of the study. Nevertheless, it is difficult to determine what kind of selection may have taken place, or if it impacted our results. It is possible that inmates who could not read were discouraged from participating in the self-administered survey. Furthermore, it is also likely that "uncooperative" inmates declined, and that inmates on certain restrictions were unable to participate. Finally, prior experience tells us that some unit administrators probably did not inform the inmates housed in their unit about the data collection each time the researchers were there to collect data. Given these factors, and others that remain unknown but which are peculiar to that day in that institution, we hesitate to provide a "response rate" because we have no idea how many inmates were actually aware that the survey was being administered and chose not to participate. Nevertheless, the most conservative response rate would be 24% (726 inmate responses divided by the maximum capacity of 3,000), though the true response rate is likely higher.

Data collection regarding socially disapproved behavior presents researchers with many challenges; perhaps most salient is the threat of a social desirability bias. The current study acknowledges that the threat of social desirability bias is heightened particularly in a correctional institution whereby respondents might feel threatened by the watchful eye of correctional employees and other inmates. Although numerous measures were taken to insure subjects of the anonymity and confidentially of all data, the threat of a social desirability bias must be acknowledged.

Nevertheless, this sample, however haphazard it may be, is uniquely suited to address issues of imprisonment and decision-making among criminal offenders. Certainly we would argue that our respondents are better suited to answer questions about the experience of criminal justice sanctions and their impact on criminal decision-making than a sample of high school or college students or a sample of non-offending adults in the general population. Although deterrence theory is a general theory of crime that should predict the decision-making processes of all individuals, the extension to a sample of incarcerated offenders provides information with important implications for policy. Data collection in correctional institutions is fraught with special restrictions and procedures, but we feel that the richness of the data in our sample counters concerns about how representative it might be.

## Dependent Variables

We included two distinct dependent variables in this effort, one associated with the gambler's fallacy and the other, with the positive punishment effect. First, respondents gauged their perceived certainty of being arrested if they were to commit a similar crime upon release (certainty, where 0 = not at all likely and 10 = very likely). This measure addressed the gambler's fallacy. Second, respondents provided a measure of intention to commit future crimes after release, allowing a test of the positive punishment/deterrence claim. Because we wanted to minimize inmates' reluctance to project their own future intentions of offending—particularly while under correctional supervision—inmates were asked to respond to the following question: "Imagine someone like yourself will be released next week. Using the number line below, please circle the likelihood that within three years that person will commit another crime." Response categories for this item ranged from 0 (not at all likely) to 10 (very likely). Respondents were asked to circle the number from 0 to 10 that best represented the likelihood of re-offending by "someone like yourself." We feel this question wording allowed inmates to respond more truthfully in terms of how they evaluated their own likelihood of re-offending upon release while at the same time providing them "cover" from any imagined response from correctional authorities. The aim of this strategy is to allow inmates to respond more truthfully without fear of reprisal or self-implication. This indirect method has been used and endorsed in previous work (see for example Bouffard, 2002; Grasmick and Bursik, 1990; Klepper and Nagin, 1989). Note that, despite the conditions under which the survey was administered, more than 50% of respondents voiced some likelihood of re-offending (where likelihood of re-offending is greater than 0).

## Independent Variables

Independent variables included perceived certainty of arrest, perceived severity of future punishment (years in prison), seven different measures of past punishment experiences, and socio-demographic control variables. When predicting intentions to re-offend, we used perceived certainty of arrest and perceived severity of future punishment as predictors to test for either a deterrent or positive punishment effect. The item measuring perceived certainty of arrest read as follows: "If you commit another crime after you are released, what is the likelihood that you will be arrested for committing that crime?" Responses for this item ranged from "0 = Not at all likely" to "10 = Very likely." The item measuring perceived severity of future punishment read as follows: "Suppose you are released from prison and are arrested again for committing a crime like the one that put you here in prison. How much time do you think you will be given?" Respondents indicated their answer in years.

Because no consensus exists regarding the preferred way to measure punishment experiences, a range of correctional punishment indicators were used. These included the following seven indicators of past punishment experience:

whether the respondent served time in a juvenile facility, whether the respondent served time in an adult correctional facility prior to the current incarceration, total months served in adult prisons and jails prior to current incarceration, total months served of current sentence, longest stretch ever served at one time (months), total months ever served in adult prisons and jails, and number of alternative sanctions ever served. In addition to correctional experience indicators, we included the following socio-demographic measures in our multivariate analyses: respondent's age (years), gender, education (years), race (White/Black), and marital status.

# Findings

Descriptive statistics for the sample are presented in Tables 7.1 and 7.2. The "average" respondent was a high school dropout with 11 years of formal education, approximately 33 years old, and had spent almost 15 months incarcerated prior to the current incarceration. We concluded data collection with 726 completed surveys, including data from 363 males and 363 females (females were over-sampled to produce about the same number of men as women), 433 Blacks, and 273 Whites. The 363 completed female surveys represented approximately 30% of all female inmates at that correctional facility, and the 363 completed male surveys represented approximately 22% of the total male inmate population at that facility. Two in three (63.7%) inmates at the institution were Black, while our sample was 60.1% Black, and 35.4% of inmates at the institution were White while our sample was 37.9% White. After deleting 20 non-White/non-Black respondents from subsequent analyses, our sample registered 433 Blacks (61.3%) and 273 Whites (38.7%). As such, the respondents providing data for this study roughly matched the inmate population at the institution with regard to both race and gender. Two in five respondents (41.4%) were incarcerated for a personal crime while one in three respondents was presently serving time for a drug-related conviction. Approximately equal percentages were married/living with someone (34.9%), separated/divorced/widowed (29.2%), and single/never married (35.9%) immediately prior to their incarceration. Most had children and four in five had experienced some form of alternative sanction.

We also collected a range of information about respondents' experience with criminal justice sanctions (Table 7.2). These include: total months spent in adult correctional centers or jail before the current incarceration (mean = 14.82 months), amount of current sentence served to date (mean = 23 months),

## Table 7.1  Sample Characteristics (N=726)

| Variable | N | % |
| --- | --- | --- |
| Gender | | |
| Male | 363 | 50.0 |
| Female | 363 | 50.0 |
| Race | | |
| Black | 433 | 61.3 |
| White | 273 | 38.7 |
| Previously Served Time in Prison | | |
| Yes | 407 | 56.1 |
| No | 318 | 43.9 |
| Current Primary Conviction | | |
| Personal | 280 | 41.4 |
| Property/Other | 147 | 21.8 |
| Drug | 294 | 36.8 |
| Have Children | | |
| Yes | 548 | 76.1 |
| No | 172 | 23.9 |
| Marital Status | | |
| Married/Living with someone | 243 | 34.9 |
| Separated/Divorced/Widowed | 203 | 29.2 |
| Never married/Single | 250 | 35.9 |
| Experienced alternative sanctions | | |
| Yes | 590 | 81.7 |
| No | 132 | 18.3 |

longest stretch of time ever served in prison at one time (months), and total time ever served in adult correctional centers or jails (months) including time served on current sentence. We were not surprised to see that current sentences appeared longer than those served in the past given that the state in which this research was conducted implemented a Truth-In-Sentencing (TIS) law in July 1995 that required all offenders sentenced after that date to serve at least 85% of their court appointed sentence. Since TIS was enacted offenders have served longer sentences than previously. In addition, respondents provided measures of perceived severity of future sanctions (the number of years the respondent thinks he/she will be given if they are released and subsequently arrested for committing a crime "like the one that put you here in prison"), and perceived like-

Table 7.2  Descriptive Statistics for Punishment Indicators
and Predictor Variables

| Variable | N | Mean | S.D. | Range |
|---|---|---|---|---|
| Age of respondent | 721 | 32.54 | 8.84 | 17-61 |
| Education | 721 | 11.25 | 2.12 | 3-18 |
| Certainty | 690 | 5.72 | 4.27 | 0-10 |
| Severity* | 608 | 25.03 | 31.41 | 0-100 |
| Total months in prison/jail prior in current incarceration | 701 | 14.82 | 30.30 | 0-264 |
| Months of current sentence served | 708 | 22.69 | 29.62 | 0-264 |
| Longest stretch served at one time (months) | 712 | 26.24 | 30.62 | 0-264 |
| Total months ever served in adult prisons/jails** | 689 | 36.96 | 43.01 | 0-462 |
| Number of alternative sanctions ever served | 722 | 2.04 | 1.84 | 0-11 |
| Likelihood to re-offend (all cases) | 716 | 2.39 | 3.15 | 0-10 |

* We assigned 100 years to respondents who predicted they would receive a life sentence.
** Combination of total months served prior to current incarceration and total month served on current sentence.

lihood of being arrested if they were to commit a similar crime upon release (certainty, where 0 = not at all likely and 10 = very likely).

# Multivariate Results

To test for the gambler's fallacy, in Table 7.3 we regressed perceived certainty of arrest on several socio-demographic indicators and seven different measures of punishment experience. We entered the seven measures of punishment experience independently because there is some overlap between several of them (for example, total months ever served in prison/jail is the sum of total months in prison/jail prior to the current incarceration plus months of current sentence served). Three of the socio-demographic indicators had a significant association with perceived certainty in each of the eight models in Table 7.3. Net of the effect of other predictors, being Male and Black tended to decrease perceived certainty, while greater education increased perceived certainty. Note that only two measures of punishment experience had significant associations with perceived certainty (months of current sentence served and longest stretch ever served at one time), and contrary to the gambler's fal-

Table 7.3  Perceived Certainty of Arrest Regressed on Socio-Demographics and Measures of Punishment Experience (Standardized Coefficients, OLS Regression)

| Predictors | Model 1 | Model 2 | Model 3 | Model 4 | Model 5 | Model 6 | Model 7 | Model 8 |
|---|---|---|---|---|---|---|---|---|
| Age (years) | -.017 | -.026 | -.018 | -.026 | -.039 | -.051 | -.049 | -.019 |
| Male | -.247** | -.247** | -.237** | -.252** | -.233** | -.243** | -.255** | -.248*** |
| Education (years) | .109** | .100** | .115** | .111** | .112** | .114** | .116** | .108*** |
| Black | -.127** | -.126** | -.118** | -.122** | -.130** | -.131** | -.120** | -.128*** |
| Married/Living With | -.001 | -.002 | -.018 | -.008 | -.005 | .003 | -.011 | -.002 |
| Separated/Divorced/Widowed | .071 | .072 | .064 | .070 | .069 | .076 | .074 | .072 |
| Served Time in a Juvenile Facility | | -.043 | | | | | | |
| Served Time in an Adult Facility Prior to Current Incarceration | | | .000 | | | | | |
| Months in Prison/Jail Prior to Current Incarceration | | | | .012 | | | | |
| Months of Current Sentence Served | | | | | .091* | | | |
| Longest Stretch Served at One Time (Months) | | | | | | .102** | | |
| Total Months Ever Served in Prison/Jail | | | | | | | .071 | |
| Number of Alternative Sanctions Ever Served | | | | | | | | .002 |
| r-square/adjusted r-square | .106/.097 | .108/.098 | .100/.089 | .106/.095 | .112/.102 | .114/.104 | .109/.099 | .106/.096 |

Reference Categories: Female, White, Single/Never Married.

*   Significant at p<.05 (two-tailed)
**  Significant at p<.01 (two-tailed)

lacy, these appear to increase perceived certainty. According to the gambler's fallacy, these measures of past punishment should be negatively correlated with perceptions of certainty of punishment. Consequently, we find no evidence to support the gambler's fallacy in this sample of incarcerated offenders.

As noted in the section titled "Dependent Variables," we also employed perceived severity of future punishment as an outcome measure. Results of this analysis are not presented here, but, not surprisingly, each of the seven measures of punishment experience generated a positive effect on perceived severity of future punishment (four of these were significant at p<.01). As this finding does not specifically address either the gambler's fallacy claim or the positive punishment claim, we decided not to include these results in table form, though they are relevant to the manner in which prior punishment experience influences perceptions of future punishment and are available from the authors upon request.

To test for a positive punishment effect, we regressed likelihood to re-offend on several socio-demographic indicators, perceived certainty and severity, and the seven different measures of punishment experience (Table 7.4). Blacks and those who were married/living with someone (compared to being single/never married) were the only two demographic predictors that had a significant impact on likelihood to re-offend. Net of the effect of other predictors, being Black generally increased the likelihood of re-offending (p<.05 in five of nine models) while being married/living with someone (compared to being single/never married) generally decreased likelihood to re-offend (p<.05 in six of nine models). With regard to measures of punishment experience, four of seven registered significant positive associations with likelihood to re-offend net of the effect of other predictors: having served time in a juvenile facility (beta = .105*), having served time in an adult facility prior to the current incarceration (beta = .167**), months in prison/jail prior to the current incarceration (beta = .162**), and the number of alternative sanctions ever served (beta = .197**). Also worth noting is that perceived certainty and severity have virtually no impact on likelihood to re-offend in any of the nine models in Table 7.4, a finding that refutes claims associated with deterrence (i.e., the manner in which sanction experiences and risk perceptions influence decisions to re-offend). Results in Table 7.4 show that past punishment experienced by respondents (juvenile and adult, custodial and non-custodial) generally increased their likelihood of re-offending, which we interpret as evidence of a positive punishment effect.

It seems logical that participation in alternative sanctions is an indicator of prior punishment, but indicators of alternative sanction experience are typically absent from deterrence studies. We argue that experience serving alternative

Table 7.4  Likelihood To Re-offend Regressed (OLS) on Socio-Demographics, Perceived Certainty and Severity, and Measures of Punishment Experience (Standardized Coefficients)

| Predictors | Model 1 | Model 2 | Model 3 | Model 4 | Model 5 | Model 6 | Model 7 | Model 8 | Model 9 |
|---|---|---|---|---|---|---|---|---|---|
| Age (years) | -.031 | -.037 | -.015 | -.052 | -.083 | -.028 | -.029 | -.063 | -.032 |
| Male | .059 | .080 | .081 | .052 | .031 | .072 | .088 | .062 | .058 |
| Education (years) | -.068 | -.057 | -.043 | -.034 | -.044 | -.053 | -.054 | -.048 | -.048 |
| Black | .100* | .086* | .082 | .087 | .092* | .089* | .089 | .084 | .094* |
| Married/Living With | -.090* | -.103* | -.106* | -.110* | -.090 | -.117* | -.107 | -.101 | -.113* |
| Separated/Divorced/Widowed | .013 | .005 | .007 | -.001 | .009 | -.005 | -.003 | -.003 | .005 |
| Perceived Severity of Future Punishment (years) | | -.002 | -.001 | .007 | -.026 | .041 | .015 | -.021 | .005 |
| Perceived Certainty of Arrest | | -.006 | -.009 | -.003 | -.001 | -.003 | .000 | -.007 | -.003 |
| Served Time in a Juvenile Facility | | | .105* | | | | | | |
| Served Time in an Adult Facility Prior to Current Incarceration | | | | .167* | | | | | |
| Months in Prison/Jail Prior to Current Incarceration | | | | | .162* | | | | |
| Months of Current Sentence Served | | | | | | -.092 | | | |
| Longest Stretch Served at One Time (Months) | | | | | | | -.036 | | |
| Total Months Ever Served in Prison/Jail | | | | | | | | .071 | |
| Number of Alternative Sanctions Ever Served | | | | | | | | | .197* |
| | | | | | | | | | |
| r-square | .029 | .030 | .041 | .058 | .052 | .038 | .032 | .034 | .068 |

Reference Categories: Female, White, Single/Never Married.

\* Significant at p<.05 (two-tailed)

\*\* Significant at p<.01 (two-tailed)

Table 7.5 Likelihood To Re-offend (0=no likelihood, 1=some likelihood) Regressed on Socio-Demographics, Perceived Certainty and Severity, and Measures of Punishment Experience (Exp. (B) Coefficients, Binary Logistic Regression)

| Predictors | M1 | M2 | M3 | M4 | M5 | M6 | M7 | M8 | M9 |
|---|---|---|---|---|---|---|---|---|---|
| Age (years) | .992 | .992 | .997 | .988 | .979 | .995 | .994 | .986 | .993 |
| Male | 1.435* | 1.405* | 1.401* | 1.283 | 1.085 | 1.346 | 1.422* | 1.269 | 1.299 |
| Education (years) | .953 | .953 | .962 | .967 | .961 | .953 | .954 | .956 | .959 |
| Black | 1.317 | 1.280 | 1.289 | 1.279 | 1.319 | 1.335 | 1.320 | 1.269 | 1.340 |
| Married/Living With | .758 | .735 | .738 | .739 | .794 | .716 | .741 | .780 | .695 |
| Separated/Divorced/Widowed | 1.061 | 1.048 | 1.074 | 1.039 | 1.088 | 1.020 | 1.031 | 1.036 | 1.055 |
| Perceived Severity of Future Punishment (years) | | .997 | .996 | .997 | .995 | 1.000 | .998 | .995 | .997 |
| Perceived Certainty of Arrest | | .991 | .994 | .989 | .995 | .995 | .994 | .993 | .993 |
| Served Time in a Juvenile Facility | | | 1.662* | | | | | | |
| Served Time in an Adult Facility Prior to this Incarceration | | | | 1.962** | | | | | |
| Months in Prison/Jail Prior to this Incarceration | | | | | 1.015** | | | | |
| Months of Current Sentence Served | | | | | | .993* | | | |
| Longest Stretch Served at One Time (Months) | | | | | | | .998 | | |
| Total Months Ever Served in Prison/Jail | | | | | | | | 1.004 | |
| Number of Alternative Sanctions Served | | | | | | | | | 1.267** |
| Cox&Snell r2/ | .021/ | .024/ | .033/ | .050/ | .056/ | .031/ | .025/ | .027/ | .064/ |
| Nagelkerke r2 | .028 | .033 | .044 | .066 | .074 | .042 | .033 | .036 | .086 |

Reference Categories:   Female, White, Single/Never Married.
* Significant at p<.05 (two-tailed)

sanctions should be taken into account because the number of offenders who have served alternative sanctions vastly outnumbers those who have been incarcerated in both our sample and in the overall population of offenders under criminal justice supervision. Currently, of the nearly 7.4 million offenders under some form of criminal justice supervision in the U.S., about 5.1 million are serving an alternative sanction. As mentioned previously, some 80% of our respondents claim to have served at least one alternative and nearly 30% have served at least three different alternatives. Because roughly 56% of respondents voiced some intention to re-offend (and conversely about 44% voiced no intention to re-offend), we also conducted binary logistic regression after dichotomizing our measure of respondents' likelihood to re-offend. In Table 7.5 the dependent variable is coded 1 for some likelihood to re-offend and 0 for no likelihood to re-offend.

In the nine models presented in Table 7.5, being male was the only sociodemographic measure with a significant impact on likelihood to re-offend. Being male increased the likelihood of reoffending in each model, although the association was statistically significant in only four of the models. Of the seven measures of punishment experience, four had a significant association with likelihood to re-offend and having served time in an adult facility prior to the current incarceration nearly doubled the odds in favor of re-offending. The only discordant note in Table 7.5 is the small negative effect associated with months of current sentence served which appears to decrease likelihood to re-offend. Again, note the positive and significant impact of experience serving alternative sanctions, the most common punishment given to convicted adult offenders. A review of multivariate results shows no support for the gambler's fallacy (Table 7.3) and generally consistent support for the positive punishment effect (Tables 7.4 and 7.5).

# Evidence for a Criminogenic Effect

This exploration of the gambler's fallacy and the positive punishment effect may raise more questions than it answers, but given our lack of knowledge about how correctional punishment influences decision-making and subsequent behaviors among habitual adult offenders, it seems appropriate to approach the issue at a very basic level. Though results are limited to simple linear and logistic regression analyses, it appears that the specific measurement of punishment experience is important when considering its effect (i.e., juvenile or adult, past or present, first or multiple incarcerations, custodial or non-custodial). Furthermore, given the impact of gender, race, and education in Table 7.3 and race and marital status in Table 7.4, it appears that the gambler's fallacy (if indeed it exists at all) and a positive punishment effect may vary by a variety of individual, family, correctional experience, and community-related items. In our analyses, being Male or Black serves to decrease perceived certainty in each of the eight models displayed while years of education increased perceived certainty (Table 7.3), even when controlling for the different punishment experience indicators. Results imply that perceived certainty was only weakly related to punishment experience (and in the opposite direction to that suggested by the gambler's fallacy), but strongly related to gender, race, and education. Being Black had a weak but significant positive impact on likelihood to re-offend in five of the nine models in Table 7.4 (OLS regression), but failed to achieve significance in Table 7.5 (logistic regression). Being Male had no significant effect on likelihood in Table 7.4, but achieved significance in four of the nine models in Table 7.5. Finally, being married or living with someone significantly reduced likelihood to re-offend in six of nine models in Table 7.4.

Based on our results, an observed positive punishment effect could not be accounted for by the gambler's fallacy or "resetting" of one's sanction-certainty estimate effect for two reasons. First, we found no empirical support for the gambler's fallacy, as only two measures of punishment experience were significantly associated with perceived certainty—but in the opposite direction to that predicted by the fallacy. Second, perceived certainty had a negligible effect on likelihood to re-offend.

With regard to a criminogenic effect, four measures of past punishment experience (having served time in a juvenile facility, having served time in an adult facility prior to the current incarceration, total months served in adult prisons/jails prior to the current incarceration, and number of alterative sanctions ever served) increased likelihood to re-offend when controlling for other relevant predictors in both OLS and logistic regression results. According to deterrence theory "Individuals who have been punished should be less inclined to offend than individuals who have not" (Pogarsky and Piquero, 2003, p. 95). While our results are far from conclusive, they mitigate in favor of a criminogenic effect. But the primary question remains: Why would prior punishment serve to increase re-offending along the lines of the positive punishment effect, and what is it about the experience of correctional punishment that might promote re-offending?

Though the direction of our results is quite consistent, our analyses routinely explain less than 10% of the variance in perceived certainty and likelihood to re-offend in this sample of incarcerated men and women. Clearly there are other important factors that must account for the remaining unexplained variation. In the case of persons who have already demonstrated a history of offending and who have experienced criminal justice sanctions, the issue narrows to that of specific deterrence, and decision-making among persons who live a criminal lifestyle.

The study of actual thought processes voiced by active criminals when considering the pros and cons of offending is found primarily in ethnographic studies of repeat and/or incarcerated offenders, and this body of work highlights concerns other than formal legal sanctions. By drawing on ethnographic accounts of criminal behavior and thought processes, it is possible to incorporate the emotions and moods of real-life offenders, which often render them unconcerned about risks traditionally entertained in traditional deterrence and rational choice models (see Bennett & Wright, 1984; Fleisher, 1995; Tunnell, 1992, 2000; Wright & Decker, 1994 for examples).

Ethnographic research suggests that persons involved in a criminal lifestyle can be said to live in a subculture with unique cultural attributes, values, rationalizations, definitions, and normative systems that set them apart from the dominant culture. For example, ethnographic work stresses the importance among street criminals of maintaining a reputation and respect among peers. "Doing crime" successfully is a way of gaining respect among like-minded colleagues. In the world of academia, publishing an article in a high quality peer-reviewed journal is presumed to generate a positive reputation and engender respect from colleagues. Likewise, successful completion of a profitable crime can be seen as adding to one's criminal vitae. Recounting how it was done and what was gained from it contributes to this process of gaining respect from others. This seems particularly likely when one's primary reference group is comprised of other habitual offenders among whom success at crime can generate greater status. Conversely, a reference group of non-criminal peers or relatives would not be disposed to confer respect on a member who has committed crime—rather that person would more likely be negatively sanctioned through shaming, embarrassment, a loss of respect from others, and possible commitment costs (job opportunities for example).

It seems likely, therefore, that as one becomes "more criminal" and spends more time with other criminals, one's primary reference group may shift from one that rewards conformity to one that is more likely to reward criminality, and an individual's own assessment of costs and benefits associated with crime will also change. This shift would seem complete among recidivists who have spent considerable time serving correctional sanctions, and who live and interact with other offenders on a relatively constant basis. In reference to active property offenders, Tunnell (2000) notes that:

... culture, or more precisely subculture, accounts for much of their activity, decision-making, and commitment to criminal careers and street life ... to better understand the nuances of repetitive property offenders, we must understand the cultures they construct through interactions with both thieves and straights and within which they function (p. 42).

Brezina and Piquero (2003) point to a voluminous literature that establishes the fact that prior crime/delinquency is the strongest predictor of future crime/delinquency and this association overshadows the effect of theoretically relevant predictors in most work. Given this, it seems important to determine just what it is about doing crime that contributes to more of it. One approach is to explore the immediate pleasures and affective sensations anticipated and experienced by criminals when and after they commit crimes. "What is lacking is adequate attention to the specific qualities of the deviant experience, the manner in which these qualities affect the offender, and the power of such qualities to motivate future criminal and delinquent behavior" (Brezina & Piquero, 2003, p. 267). Perhaps a positive punishment effect can be best explained by the pursuit of a criminal lifestyle and the benefits/rewards that habitual criminals associate with offending, and that individuals become more criminal or incorrigible through "experiential learning" from other offenders in a correctional environment (Akers & Sellers, 2004; Bandura, 1977; Stafford & Warr, 1993). In this way the experience of prison or other correctional sanctions may serve as a sort of "professional development seminar" of uncertain duration that results in stronger commitment to the pursuit of crime.

This explanation seems closely aligned with social learning theory and the manner in which positive reinforcers promote repeat behavior. Learning theory would argue that as offenders become more integrated into a criminal lifestyle, they absorb and internalize definitions about costs and benefits associated with crime that they learn from other offenders. It is likely, then, that a range of reinforcers may come to be viewed as beneficial among delinquents through interaction with more experienced offenders who have already learned to interpret their effects as positive and worth pursuing. This implies that, among a group of experienced criminal offenders, the presumed intrinsic nonsocial reinforcement of deviance is enhanced or "supercharged" by socially learning to interpret the psychological and/or physiological effect as good through peer association. The process mirrors Becker's (1953) classic explanation of how one becomes a regular marijuana user by learning to experience the effects of the drug as pleasurable through interaction with other regular users (see also Topalli, 2005, Topalli, 2006).

# Implications for Theory

One of the more obvious shortcomings in deterrence/rational choice research is the paucity of work that expressly incorporates benefits associated with "doing crime." One might suspect that offenders must gain something from doing crimes—otherwise they would not regularly offend, even after experiencing both informal and formal sanctions resulting from their offenses. Models presented in Tables 7.4 and 7.5 are only marginally effective in explaining likelihood to re-offend, and a vast amount of variation is left unexplained. As such, a consideration of benefits (reinforcers) that may *motivate* such behavior seems fruitful.

Motivation is an essential dimension of criminal decision-making, and researchers are naturally interested in motivation "... because it represents a component of the decision problem: the benefits and calculable results the decision maker anticipates from engaging in a particular act" (Tunnell, 1992, p. 39). Ethnographic accounts offered by active offenders regularly speak of the fun, thrills, challenge, sense of accomplishment, respect, exhilaration, money, property, revenge, power, and other "rewards" associated with doing crimes and living a criminal lifestyle. Recent integration of rational choice and traditional deterrence perspectives has produced a more comprehensive understanding of offender decision-making, but does not account for important motivational processes discussed above. The operationalization and inclusion of motivating factors common to ethnographic accounts of active offenders would seem to hold much promise in furthering our understanding of offender decision-making.

Non-social reinforcers have a powerful impact on human behavior and on the thought processes of criminal offenders, and deserve to be included in quantitative models of offender decision-making (Wood et al., 1997). We propose that a criminogenic effect is likely caused by social and non-social reinforcements generated by doing crime and prolonged and intimate contact with other offenders while serving correctional sanctions, both of which increase the likelihood of re-offending. In addition, those with reentry experience know that the barriers to reintegration faced by returning offenders are formidable, and there is a strong likelihood that such barriers will eventually channel them into re-offending. These barriers include issues related to a host of "invisible punishments" (i.e., problems with employment, housing, welfare assistance, voter disenfranchisement, etc.), the stigma attached to ex-convicts and probation/parole supervision that result in high rates of revocation (Mauer & Chesney-Lind, 2002). Significant obstacles to reintegration are yet another reason why offenders who have experienced prior punishment and release are very likely to re-offend. In sum, a positive punishment or criminogenic effect is likely due to at least three factors; a) the social and non-social "seductions of crime"; b) the positive punishment effect of formal sanctions as manifested in "experiential learning" in a correctional environment; and c) diminished reentry opportunities, all of which combine to promote re-offending. At this stage it is impossible to determine which of these carries greater weight, and future research should examine this confluence of factors using multivariate designs that operationalize them. As the United States has pursued a policy of mass imprisonment for nearly three decades, now boasts the highest incarceration rate in the world, and returns over 700,000 ex-convicts into communities each year, more attention to this issue is warranted—particularly because it could be argued that, for many offenders, criminal justice punishments may promote future offending.

## CHAPTER 8

# IMPLICATIONS FOR POLICY, RESEARCH, AND THEORIES OF OFFENDER DECISION-MAKING

The growth of the U.S. prison population is unmatched in human history, but it hasn't been the largest area of growth in the criminal justice system. While imprisonment has been in the spotlight, the number of people on probation or parole has quietly surged to more than 5 million, up from 1.6 million just 25 years ago. One in 45 adults in the United States is now under community supervision, and, combined with those in prison and jail, 1 in every 31 (3.2 % of American adults) is under some form of correctional control. The rates are higher for men (1 in 18) and Blacks (1 in 11) and are even higher in some states (1 in 13 in Georgia) and up to 1 in 7 adult males in some high-crime urban neighborhoods (PEW, 2009).

Community corrections programs have had much larger population growth than prisons but far smaller budget growth. Among state correctional systems, eight times as many new dollars went to prisons as went to probation and parole. And while only about 30% of offenders are incarcerated, almost 90% of corrections dollars are spent on prisons. It is true that incarceration costs more, and prisons must house, feed and care for the most dangerous offenders. But the price gap between prison and community-based sanctions is enormous. In 2008 the average daily cost of supervising a probationer in the community was $3.42 while the average daily cost of a prison inmate was $78.95—more than 20 times as high (PEW, 2009). Community corrections agencies have absorbed an additional 3.5 million offenders since 1980, and this increase has come without commensurate investments in staff, equipment and other support.

Despite meager funding and expanded responsibilities, there have been fundamental advances in community supervision. New and more discriminating risk assessment tools work better to determine which offenders pose the greatest risk to the community, which ones require the most supervision, and what sort of monitoring and services they need. Global positioning system devices, rapid-result drug tests, greater use of computer-assisted monitoring, and other new technologies are able to track offenders' whereabouts and behavior. Offender supervision, treatment, and re-entry programs are incorporating solid research on how to cut recidivism. Performance incentives are increasingly available for both offenders and community supervision agencies, and agencies are doing a better job tracking new arrests, collection of victim restitution and other key outcomes. Taken together, these approaches can produce real reductions in recidivism and save money along the way—a claim that cannot be made with regard to imprisonment. However, if these results are to be sustained and expanded across jurisdictions, significant investments must be made in community corrections. Enhancements in community corrections can cut crime and reduce the need not only for new prisons but even for some existing facilities. The savings—estimated at approximately $75 per offender per day—could be diverted to reinforce probation and parole, fund pre-release programs, support early-intervention strategies, and invest in the troubled neighborhoods from which most prisoners originate and return to, resulting in further reductions in crime and imprisonment.

## Deficits in Community Corrections Research

In the mid-1990s, the majority of directors of local and state criminal justice agencies identified alternative sanctions as the top priority for research and evaluation (NIJ, 1995). Unfortunately, this charge has not been addressed sufficiently in the research literature. For example, until quite recently (1999), only five studies of inmate perceptions of sanction severity had been published, and except for two of these (Petersilia & Deschenes 1994a, 1994b; Spelman, 1995), the small number of studies did not included many newer alternative sanctions (i.e., day fine, electronic monitoring, intermittent incarceration, day reporting). In addition, researchers often reached conclusions based on only a small sample of offenders. Petersilia and Deschenes (1994b), for example, based their entire analysis on just 48 male inmate respondents. While this might be sufficient for a pilot study, analysis of inmate subgroups rapidly exhausts the sample and precludes the researcher from meaningful group comparisons. Third, while all inmates have personal experience with imprisonment, previous studies had failed to control for personal experience in serving alternative sanctions. To arrive at a valid offender ranking of alternatives compared to imprisonment it would seem preferable to survey inmates who had personal experience serving *both* traditional prison sentences and the alternatives in question. While it is true that the particulars of alternative sanctions become well known to inmates who have not experienced them, such second-hand information is potentially less valid than information from offenders with first-hand knowledge and experience. Fourth, previous research has ignored group differences. The gender, race, and correctional experience comparisons we provide in Chapters 4 and 7 provide a first glimpse at gender, race, and correctional experience differences in how inmates rank the severity of alternatives compared to prison and how they respond to correctional sanctions in terms of risk perceptions and intentions to re-offend. For example, with the rapid rise in female inmate populations, examination of female perceptions of sanction severity, risk perceptions, and intentions to re-offend would seem useful. If women are significantly more amenable to alternative sanctions, their enrollment might be increased, saving prison space and financial resources. Fifth, though anecdotal evidence abounds, previous work has failed to systematically investigate why a large proportion of inmates eligible for alternatives choose to avoid them. Interestingly, findings presented here show that reasons for avoiding or participating in such sanctions have little to do with the specifics of the program or the institution in which inmates are serving time (i.e., program rules too strict, prison too harsh on inmates), but have much to do with the manner in which such programs are administered, specifically; 1) the conduct and personalities of parole and probation officers and program administrators, and 2) the high failure and revocation rates associated with many alternative sanctions. These findings support speculations entertained by prior research (Fleischer, 1995; Petersilia & Deschenes 1994a, 1994b; Spelman, 1995), and the conclusions of deterrence/rational choice scholars that "indirect" sanctions or costs may generate a greater deterrent effect than direct sanctions (Grasmick & Bursik, 1990; Williams & Hawkins, 1986, Williams & Hawkins, 1989). Finally, there is very little research that explores how the experience of correctional sanctions conditions offenders for re-entry into society, and whether such experiences may inhibit or promote re-offending.

# Issues Associated With Deterrence and Offender Decision-Making

Our findings bear directly on issues of deterrence and offender decision-making, and offer some data-driven reasons for why deterrence may not work for many offenders. The fact that inmates with prison experience view alternatives as more punitive than prison brings into question the value of brief imprisonment as a specific deterrent. Findings presented here show that many inmates would rather serve a brief prison term than most of the alternatives, and many inmates view a brief prison term as an opportunity to relax away from the pressures of surviving on the street. Several inmates interviewed by the authors noted that the brief term they were to serve would give them the opportunity to have some dental work done at the expense of the state. Others appreciated the regular meals and shelter and a chance to "chill out" and see old friends. Clearly, a brief prison stay has little or no deterrent value for these persons, and such a sanction even has its attractive features for many offenders. For them, imprisonment is more predictable than alternative sanctions. Relatedly, interviews with long-term inmates substantiate the idea that those who spend significant time in correctional facilities become "institutionalized"—a consequence highlighted in films like "The Shawshank Redemption" and in a range of books and monographs penned by inmates serving long prison terms (Rideau, Santos, etc.). Such inmates are typically unprepared for re-entry and voice considerable anxiety about leaving an environment to which they have adapted their lives. Inmates in their 50s, 60s, and 70s have few viable options for housing, employment, and health care once released, and family and community support systems have often atrophied or disappeared over the years of their imprisonment. For these inmates, release is often a prelude to misery and potential re-offending. More than one has voiced trepidation regarding imminent release, and had intentions to re-offend in order to facilitate their return to what they perceive as a "safe," preferred prison environment that offers them shelter, sustenance, a modicum of healthcare, and familiar faces and routines.

Perhaps most damning to a specific deterrence claim, however, is evidence presented in Chapter 7. Analysis of survey data from over 700 incarcerated men and women refutes the gambler's fallacy proposed by some scholars by finding that punishment experiences have no impact on risk perceptions, that risk perceptions had no impact on intentions to re-offend, and that greater punishment experience appears to increase likelihood of recidivism after release. The observed positive punishment effect is associated with having experienced both custodial and non-custodial sanctions. These findings suggest considerable support for a criminogenic effect of correctional punishments rather than a deterrent effect. While this might seem surprising, consider that at least two-thirds of released offenders are re-arrested within three years, and it is likely that the majority of the remaining third has also offended but simply hasn't been caught—yet. Given the extremely high recidivism and re-arrest rates among those who have experienced correctional punishments, and the revolving door nature of prison admissions and releases, isn't it more reasonable to assume a criminogenic rather than a deterrent effect?

# Gender

The observed gender differences in perceived punitiveness of sanctions discussed in Chapter 4 suggest gender differences in deterrence dynamics—particularly with regard to informal costs of imprisonment. Recall that our findings indicate that women are more amenable to alternatives, and will do more time in alternatives than will men. Women in our samples average 32 years of age and nearly 80% of them have at least one child. At the same time over 75% of these female inmates claim to be single. We assume that single women with children typically take primary responsibility for care-giving in the home—particularly child care. Such care-giving is impossible if a woman is incarcerated, but remains likely if the woman is placed in a community-based alternative sanction. Further, single mothers who are sentenced to imprisonment may often lose custody of their children, while if placed in a community-based program they may not. We believe this is one reason why women are more amenable to alternative sanctions.

In addition, most states have far fewer prisons for female offenders than for males, and many have only one such prison. Women sentenced to imprisonment may find themselves far removed (geographically) from their home communities, and distance may preclude the possibility of regular contact with children and family members. This problem is not nearly as severe for men, who may manage to serve their time in prisons or county jails in or near their home communities, and who typically do not assume primary care-giving responsibilities. There seem several "rational" reasons why women view imprisonment as more punitive than alternatives compared to men. This implies that women may employ a different "cost-benefit analysis" than men when considering criminal behavior, pointing to a possible gender difference in deterrence dynamics. Women may be more tuned to the informal costs of imprisonment than are men, and if so, women with primary care-giving duties who face imprisonment may be ideal candidates for community-based sanctions. Our findings raise an interesting question—do deterrence dynamics differ by gender?

It seems clear that female inmates respond differently to alternative sanctions than do males (Chapter 4). While the two groups generate a similar punitiveness ranking with regard to specific punishments, women appear significantly more amenable to alternatives than do men and are willing to endure longer durations of those alternatives. We suggest that gender differences in the rational-choice calculation of costs and benefits are likely to exist, and these differences may influence gender differences in deterrence dynamics. Such potential gender differences have been ignored by rational choice and deterrence scholars, but there seems evidence in their favor. Women are particularly likely to be influenced by care-giving responsibilities and correction systems offer them fewer geographic options for incarceration. Consideration of the unique needs of female inmates—particularly those with primary care-giving responsibilities—should be a primary research focus in sanction development.

## Race

With regard to race, our findings are perhaps more controversial, but placed in the appropriate context are not at all surprising. Research consistently finds that "African-Americans see the criminal justice system as racially biased; while the majority of Whites generally believe the system is racially neutral and reflects the ideal of equal treatment before the law" (Henderson et al., 1997, p. 455). Surveys and polls routinely show that a larger proportion of Blacks than of Whites have less favorable opinions about various components of justice, including police, courts, judges, juries, and lawyers (Cao et al., 1996; Roberts & Stalans, 2000; Tuch & Weitzer, 1997). According to the most recent available data, a greater proportion of Blacks than Whites have "very little" confidence in both the criminal justice system (51% v. 30%) and the police (34% v. 9%), are more likely to feel that the criminal justice system is "very unfair" in its treatment of people accused of committing crime (19% v. 9%), are more fearful that they will be stopped and arrested by the police when they are innocent (42% v. 16%), and are more likely to perceive that there is police brutality in their communities (67% v. 25%) (Maguire & Pastore, 2008). Given that these perceptions of criminal justice practitioners characterize Blacks' views of the justice system; it would not be surprising to find that many black offenders view alternative sanctions with suspicion, particularly if they expect poor treatment or discrimination by program officers and consider the risk of revocation to be high. Furthermore, if Henderson et al. (1997) are correct, suspicion regarding the community-sanctions component of criminal justice may be even more pronounced among low-income Blacks, particularly those who have already experienced arrest, conviction, and/or punishment.

Our results unambiguously show that Black offenders are less amenable to alternative sanctions than are Whites, are more likely than Whites to choose imprisonment when given a choice between prison and a range of community-based sanctions, and evidence a greater likelihood of re-offending than Whites when controlling for other demographic, risk perception, and correctional experience indicators. African-Americans now account for nearly 50% of all inmates in the U.S., and one in nine black men aged 20–34 are behind bars.

Black men today have roughly a one in three chance of going to prison in their lifetime (Bonczar, 2003).

Crouch (1993) suggests that African-Americans may adjust to prison more easily than other groups, perhaps because a large proportion of inner-city black males are imprisoned and they routinely find friends and relatives already in prison who can provide them with information, material goods, and protection. He argues that the urban underclass lifestyle makes the potential violence and deprivation of a prison term seem less threatening to Blacks compared to Whites.

> Because the ghettos from which many African-Americans come are often unpredictable and threatening environments, they learn to emphasize self-protection and to develop physical and psychological toughness. This toughness protects African-American prisoners and enables them to dominate others behind bars, especially Whites… it suggests that race and ethnicity may influence how offenders view the relative costs of punitiveness of criminal sanctions (Crouch, 1993, p. 71).

Blacks are more likely than Whites to be sent to prison, are often more familiar with what to expect in prison, and are more likely to find acquaintances there, circumstances that may make prison less threatening. For these reasons, we believe that, given a choice between prison and a range of alternative sanctions, African-Americans would choose prison more often than would Whites.

There are also other reasons to expect that Blacks are more likely than Whites to choose prison over a range of alternative sanctions. African-Americans (more than Whites) may tend to feel that they will be subject to abuse or harassment under alternative sanctions, and thus may feel they are more likely to be revoked back to prison. This implies that Blacks and Whites entertain a different "risk assessment" when it comes to evaluating whether participation in an alternative is a gamble they are willing to take. Rather than viewing prison as less punitive than alternatives, it is therefore possible that prison contains less uncertainty, and many offenders (black and white) may wish to serve out their terms and be released rather than invest time and effort in an alternative sanction involving potentially abusive program officers and a high likelihood of program violation and revocation. Questions remain, however, about whether such risk assessments vary by race, and if so, why.

Other than the work presented here, only four published works have explored race difference in perceptions of sanction severity. Petersilia and Deschenes failed to find a significant race difference. However, Crouch (1993) observed that "being African-American is the strongest predictor of a preference for prison" (p. 67) and Spelman (1995) found that "the most important predictor of preference for a jail term is the offender's race" (p. 122). Our results suggest that black probationers were more likely than Whites to choose prison over alternatives, and among offenders who were willing to serve alternatives to avoid prison, Whites would serve longer durations of them. Black offenders were also two to four times as likely as Whites to choose prison rather than serve any amount of a given alternative sanction. In our Kentucky study, the interaction of race and prior prison experience generates significant differences in severity rankings, as Blacks with prior prison experience rank prison as the seventh most punitive punishment, while white first-timers rank it as the third most punitive sanction. In sum, the evidence consistently shows that, for many offenders in general, but particularly for black offenders, imprisonment is not the most severe form of punishment.

## Correctional Experience

Our results presented here also suggest that offenders with more correctional experience are less willing to serve alternative sanctions and more likely to prefer to serve prison instead. This contradicts the idea of the traditional probation to prison severity continuum. If prison were perceived by inmates as significantly more punitive than alternatives, then persons with more prison experience should be more willing to serve alternative sanctions—and to serve longer durations of them—to avoid imprisonment. However, this is not the case. In fact, the opposite is true. Offenders who have acquired knowledge and experience about living in prison appear less fearful of prison than those without such experience. For them, prison is less of an unknown, and for some it may be seen as easier than an alternative sanction—particularly if they perceive the alternative as involving an unacceptable degree of supervision, mistreatment, and/or a high likelihood of revocation. Particularly among inmates with experience serving time, imprisonment becomes familiar, while the outcome of involvement in alternatives is less certain and less attractive. In contrast, persons without prior experience in prison may be more fearful of it, and will opt to do the alternative—and a longer duration of it—in order to avoid prison. Again, this brings into question the deterrent value of imprisonment, because those who have served prison are more likely to choose it when given the choice between prison and an alternative sanction.

While this may seem strange to those not familiar with serving time, it has been noted that most offenders would rather do a longer prison term, for example, than a short jail sentence (Fleisher, 1995). Fleisher cites an offender who says he would rather do three or four years at the State Penitentiary before doing one year in the county jail, because "It be too hard to have a good time up in that ol' jail. Now, in prison, that's different." Fleisher goes on to note, "Prison isn't a risk that worries street hustlers. Things such as limited freedom, loss of privacy, violence, and variant sexual activity, which might frighten lawful citizens, don't frighten them" (Fleisher, 1995, p. 164).

Persons with significant experience serving correctional sanctions are more familiar with and less fearful of incarceration, and view it as less severe compared to when they were first imprisoned. Experienced cons see alternatives as more of a "hassle" now, and feel more comfortable serving their time incarcerated rather than in the community. In addition, interviews with offenders serving both custodial and non-custodial sanctions reveal that experienced convicts hold alternatives in disdain. Experienced cons view those willing to subject themselves to the supervision and restrictions of alternatives as punks who are fearful of prison, and who are willing to subject themselves to "institutionalized embarrassment" in order to avoid doing time in the general prison population. For many offenders with prison experience, alternatives are a "copout" of sorts, and carry the stigma of being reserved for younger and weaker offenders.

In sum, our results suggest a more sophisticated process of "rational choice" than that traditionally presumed by most deterrence theorists (Grasmick & Bursik, 1990; Williams & Hawkins, 1986), and offer some convincing explanations for why deterrence may not apply to many (if not most) offenders serving correctional sanctions. In addition to clear gender, race, and correctional experience differences, inmates identify factors they say would cause them to avoid alternatives that have little to do with the official demands of the programs themselves. Inmates are particularly aware of the pitfalls waiting for them should they enroll in certain alternatives, but such considerations are typically ignored by policy-makers, who likely see such sanctions as opportunities that inmates should be eager to seize. Implementation of alternatives devised by legislators may be politically attractive and expedient, but in practice such reforms often have latent consequences unforeseen by policy-makers.

# Implications for Policy and Practice

Four traditional aims of punishment are rehabilitation, retribution/desert, incapacitation, and deterrence (von Hirsch and Ashworth, 1992). A 1995 survey of over 250 criminal court judges and district attorneys in Oklahoma asked them to identify the primary purpose/aim of 17 different sanctions ranging from the death penalty to various alternative sanctions (DataLinks, 1996). There was general agreement on the aim/purpose of 16 of the sanctions, but no clear agreement on the purpose of a "brief prison term." Recent evidence suggests that up to 40% of offenders entering state correctional systems receive a sentence of five years or less and are likely to serve no more than one year actual imprisonment. Given the views of judges and district attorneys, and the inmates in our surveys, the purpose of a brief prison stay seems uncertain. One solution is to restrict brief prison stays to a specific group of offenders, and sentence most non-violent offenders to an alternative sanction. This would relieve pressure on an overcrowded system and lighten the fiscal load while reducing the use of a sanction that many inmates do not take seriously and many criminal justice practitioners apparently agree is of dubious worth.

Related to the above is the question of what goals corrections systems aim to achieve, and how is success measured? In complex organizations, goals associated with a particular policy vary by individuals and organizational units. In corrections, this problem is exacerbated by the different roles units and individuals play. Duffee (1985) notes that achieving organizational goals associated with alternative sanctions (reduced overcrowding, cost effectiveness, rehabilitation, proportionate sentencing, etc.) requires the cooperation of many different units and individuals, including upper administration, facility administrators, case managers, probation and parole officers, and the offenders themselves. Nevertheless, decision-makers in different parts of the organization tend to define goals differently, which often causes conflict among employees at various levels around what the goals of the organization.

Regarding probation and parole officers, Duffee observes that two primary goals seem in conflict. First, officers are charged with maximizing benefits to offenders through counseling and casework to help them reenter society. Second, officers are charged with maximizing surveillance and community protection through enforcing rules and regulations that enhance revocation. While upper-level administrators may view alternatives as a way to reduce overcrowding and costs that provides offenders the opportunity for re-entry and rehabilitation, program officers often see alternatives as a test of their ability to restrict offender's movement in the community, and may measure success by increases in the rate of technical violations and revocations. Note that the percentage of prison admissions attributed to parole and probation violations now exceeds 40%. Consequently, inmates may see alternatives as too risky and unpredictable, and may prefer imprisonment over a community-based sanction that is too restrictive. In this case correctional management's goal involves a "decision generator" which creates a policy favorable toward alternative sanctions, while the program officers' goal may be more specific and involve increased surveillance and restriction of a probationer's movements. In practice the two goals clash, reducing the ability of both parties to achieve their goals (Duffee, 1985).

Further, achieving one goal of punishment may undermine another goal that is equally important. For example, the nationwide increase in the punitiveness of punishment through harsher and longer sentences may achieve a truer measure of retribution, but it may also undermine the utilitarian goals of deterrence and rehabilitation. Inmates may be imprisoned longer than what is necessary to deter them from further crimes, and the increased duration of imprisonment may serve a socializing function that increases the adoption of pro-crime values (the "crime school" idea). In such a scenario, deterrence and rehabilitation are sacrificed for the sake of retribution.

Not only may there be a conflict regarding goals, but goals may change over a relatively short period of time. Durham (1994) observes that in 1967 fully 73% of citizens' surveyed said rehabilitation was the primary correctional goal, while in 1982 only 44% of citizens felt the same way. By the end of the 1980s the majority of citizens viewed punishment as more important than rehabilitation, a sentiment that remains in 2009 (Innes, 1993; Pastore and McGuire, 2008). This decrease in support for rehabilitation is paralleled by an increase in the just deserts principle, which has also resulted in a shift in the kinds of evidence regarded as indicative of correctional effectiveness. Rather than judging effectiveness based on reductions in recidivism rates, it might now be judged based on increases in incarceration rates, or average duration of sentence served. Given the changes in not only the primary goals of punishment, but also in how to measure success, it is not surprising that modern correctional systems have generally been unable to achieve anything approaching the level of effectiveness hoped for by citizens, legislators, or criminal justice practitioners. For example, in the late 1960s and early 1970s Intensive Supervision Probation (ISP) was seen as incompatible with rehabilitative goals because of the high rate of technical violations due to increased surveillance of offenders on ISP, resulting in high rates of revocation back to prison. In the current climate that emphasizes punishment and incapacitation, however, ISP has become among the most widely used of all alternative sanctions, partly because it results in detection of more violations and higher rates of revocation to prison (Reichel, 1998).

# Conclusions

In their 1990 work, *Between Prison and Probation*, Morris and Tonry urged states to develop punishment equivalencies (what we call exchange rates) between traditional incarceration and a range of community-based sanctions that would allow judges to choose sentences to suit an individual offender's risk-level and personal characteristics. Results from our surveys and interviews of men and women serving both custodial and non-custodial sanctions in several states explicitly challenge the notion of a continuum of sanctions bounded by regular probation at one extreme and traditional incarceration at the other. While our findings suggest that the conventional wisdom of placing regular probation at the low end of a continuum of sanction severity may be valid, it is clear there are community-based sanctions that many if not most offenders perceive as more onerous than traditional incarceration (Crouch, 1993; Petersilia & Deschenes, 1994a, 1994b; Spelman, 1995). It is also apparent that different groups of offenders rate the severity of sanctions differently (i.e., men versus women, Whites versus Blacks, experienced cons versus first-timers, parents versus non-parents).

Though legislators and criminal justice policy-makers have operated under the assumption that a continuum like that envisioned by Morris and Tonry is valid, the reality appears more complex. Inmates with personal experience of both imprisonment and alternatives identify several alternatives they rate as more punitive than prison. Depending on the specific sanction, a significant proportion of inmates will refuse to participate in the alternative even if it means a shorter duration of imprisonment. Reservations about participating in alternatives seem to focus on: 1) the manner in which alternatives are administered—particularly concerns about abusive or antagonistic personnel who run such programs; and 2) the likelihood of program failure and revocation to prison after investing time and effort in the alternative. These concerns are significant enough to generate considerable rejection of alternatives by inmates who would rather serve out their time and be released with no strings attached.

Von Hirsch et al.'s (1992) call for the development of a theory of sentence severity that provides a foundation for a comprehensive sentencing system that incorporates both custodial and non-custodial sanctions may seem ideological and even unattainable to some. But even the longest journey begins with a single step, and Morris and Tonry note that:

> ... all that can in reality be achieved and all that should in practice be sought is a rough and ready equivalence of punishment in terms of preserving a reasonably fair and just punishment system, doing as much good as it can, and avoiding needless suffering and expense where it can (Morris & Tonry, 1990, p. 97).

We do not claim to have accomplished any of these goals, but the work presented here is a basis for incremental progress in that direction. We approached a theory of sentence severity from an offender's perspective and solicited exchange rates between a variety of intermediate sanctions and prison from prisoners, probationers, and parolees. These exchange rates allowed us to produce rankings of sanction severity, to operationalize "severity" from an offender's viewpoint, and to identify categories of factors that influence variation in these exchange rates. As intimated by Von Hirsch et al., (1992), a theory of sentence severity should not only address what is meant by severity but should also attempt to identify factors that influence how a range of sanctions are experienced and ranked.

Findings presented here cast doubt on the value of correctional sanctions as specific deterrent mechanisms. Compared to those with no imprisonment history, offenders with prior prison experience would serve less of each alternative to avoid prison and voice a greater preference for prison rather than serve any duration of an alternative. In addition, those with more punishment experience—both custodial and non-custodial—registered a greater likelihood of re-offending after release. Therefore, one might rightly question the presumed deterrent value of brief imprisonment for at least some subgroups of offenders. The significance of our findings for theories associated with deterrence and offender decision-making generates potentially provocative and controversial issues.

Some readers may misconstrue our work as promoting alternatives over prison in order to achieve a greater reduction in recidivism or crime control. The efficacy of intermediate punishments compared to imprisonment is usually rated in terms of cost and crime prevention (i.e., recidivism). In fact, though most research on intermediate sanctions determines they are generally not more effective than imprisonment in reducing future crime, it is also the case that little evidence exists to suggest that imprisonment has a greater specific deterrent effect than intermediate sanctions. Additionally, while evaluations of intermediate sanctions note that such programs are not *less* effective than imprisonment, they are potentially less *expensive* than imprisonment. As noted by Tonry (1996), "… well managed intermediate sanctions offer a cost-effective way to keep [offenders] in the community at less cost than imprisonment and with no worse later prospect for criminality" (1996, p. 132). If an alternative sanction is equally effective (or non-effective) in reducing recidivism, perceived by offenders as equally punitive, and is significantly less expensive than imprisonment, there seems good reason to expand its use.

These considerations are often ignored by legislators and policy-makers, who likely see the kinds of sanctions examined here as opportunities that inmates should be eager to seize in order to avoid incarceration. In fact, other than capital punishment, imprisonment is seen by many policy officials as the only response to crime worthy of the label "tough." Construing the matter in these terms, however, can set in motion a cycle that has been aptly captured by Clear (1994, p. 176), a cycle likely to continue as long as being tough on crime is equated almost entirely with imprisoning offenders at high rates.

> We come by our nonsensically large penal system as a product of our nonsensical political approach to crime. [Elected officials place] a premium on instituting tough politics. Each new elected generation erects its tough policies on the failed foundations of the previous group. The direction of penal harms is ever upward in scale and scope (Clear, 1994, p. 176).

Several caveats and considerations for future research relate to our findings. First, use of multivariate procedures allows a more comprehensive look at factors that influence offenders' perceptions of the severity of a range of criminal justice sanctions, and such procedures should be encouraged in future work. Second, it is important to continue to investigate factors that influence offenders' likelihood of serving alternative sanctions and those that lead offenders to avoid or choose prison. While we find that specific demographic characteristics, prior correctional experience, attitudes about intermediate sanctions, and conditions associated with the pain and suffering of imprisonment influence offenders' penal exchange rates, severity rankings, and likelihood to re-offend, the fact that we explain only a moderate amount of variation in our outcome measures suggests that there are other factors yet to be identified that play an important role. Third, the generation of larger samples across several jurisdictions and the inclusion of a wider variety of predictors would offer a better understanding of these dynamics. Our research here used offenders' responses from several states (Oklahoma, Indiana, Kentucky, and Mississippi), and we feel it is important to generate additional samples from different regions of the country to determine if variation in contextual factors associated with correctional facility, jurisdiction, or geographic location impact exchange rates as well. Multi-level models would likely improve our understanding of what influences offenders' decision-making on this issue.

Finally, the nature of the relationships discussed here is complex, and future research should include open-ended, qualitative methods to more fully understand offender-generated exchange rates, as well as group differences discussed above. Though this research is labor intensive, time consuming, and often difficult, the contribution it promises would far outweigh the difficulties experienced in collecting these types of data. Qualitative studies of these phenomena may yield an understanding of factors heretofore unexamined that impact how offenders rate the severity of correctional sanctions. Along the same line, future researchers in this area should remain aware that offenders' self-reported perceptions may not always parallel their behaviors. That is, the sanction(s) respondents would prefer in studies like ours may or may not be indicative of what they would do if given the actual choice between serving custodial and non-custodial sentences. More work is needed to develop reliable punishment exchange rates and a meaningful continuum of sanctions that can contribute to a valid theory of sentence severity.

As the popularity and application of alternative sanctions continues to grow, it behooves prosecutors, judges, and legislators to be cognizant of how offenders subjectively perceive the severity of prison when compared to alternative sanctions. By doing so, sentencing strategies based on reliable exchange rates tied to a valid theory of sentence severity could be devised that would almost certainly decrease the burden placed on taxpayers to continue funding mass imprisonment, an investment that, to date, has provided far greater dividends at exacting retribution in the minds of policy-makers and the public than at dispensing fair, proportionate, or effective punishments.

# APPENDIX A

# MEASURING EXCHANGE RATES

Below we have listed a number of correctional alternatives that people may be sentenced to instead of prison. For each one, please read the description of the program, and then follow the instructions provided.

(1). **County Jail.** If you are sent to county jail, you spend less time there than you would in prison. However, living conditions are much worse than in prison. Your freedom is very restricted, and there is less time for you to do what you want or be involved in activities. You are generally in a cell 24 hours a day, and there is usually no yard time allowed. Jail time is generally viewed as worse than prison time.

Think about 12 months actual time in a medium-security correctional center.

What is the maximum number of months of county jail you would take to avoid serving *12* months actual time in prison? (Put an X on the line below to indicate the answer.)

0    2    4    6    8    10    12    14    16    18    20    22    24

_____

The X is equal to _____ months in county jail (write the number).

**(2.) Boot Camp.** Boot camp is for a shorter time than you would have been sent to prison. But boot camp can be more unpleasant in many ways than living in prison. Boot camp is like basic training in the army. You live with about a hundred other people in one big room. There is regular drill instruction like in the military and you are pushed physically and psychologically to perform beyond your capabilities. You experience loss of sleep. You are required to become physically active and fit. You are constantly supervised by drill instructors who watch you closely. You are generally required to participate in an education program. Virtually all your time and activities are controlled. You are subject to random urinalysis tests and can be sent back to prison if you fail to obey the rules.

Think about 12 months actual time in a medium-security correctional center.

What is the maximum number of months of boot camp you would take to avoid serving *12* months actual time in prison? (Put an X on the line below to indicate the answer.)

0     2     4     6     8     10     12     14     16     18     20     22     24

_____

The X is equal to_____ months in boot camp (write the number).

(3). **Electronic Monitoring.** On electronic monitoring, you live at home, but your freedom is greatly reduced. You wear an electronic device on your ankle. If you get more than 200 feet from your telephone, the device sends an alarm to a computer. Then an officer who is supervising you knows that you are not where you are supposed to be. On electronic monitoring you are being followed by the computer 24 hours a day. There are strict curfews and rules about when you must stay near your phone. If you break these rules, you can be sent to prison. You are subject to random urinalysis tests and can be sent back to prison if you fail to obey the rules.

Think about 12 months actual time in a medium-security correctional center.

What is the maximum number of months on electronic monitoring you would take to avoid serving *12* months actual time in prison? (Put an X on the line below to indicate the answer.)

0   4   8   12   16   20   24   28   32   36   40   44   48

_____

The X is equal to _____ months in electronic monitoring (write the number).

**4). Regular Probation.** On probation, you do not spend time in prison, but the amount of time on probation usually lasts much longer than whatever prison sentence you might have gotten. You must see your probation officer at least once a month, but it can be every week if ordered. You must get permission from that probation officer to travel or to move. Your probation officer can require that you stay away from certain people. Your home or car can be searched at any time without a search warrant. If you do not follow the rules you can be sent to prison. You are also subject to random urinalysis tests.

Think about 12 months actual time in a medium-security correctional center.

What is the maximum number of months of regular probation you would take to avoid serving *12* months actual time in prison? (Put an X on the line below to indicate the answer.)

0    4    8    12    16    20    24    28    32    36    40    44    48

---

The X is equal to _____ months on regular probation (write the number).

(5). **Community Service.** When you are sentenced to community service, you live at home and can have a job. However, you must work some time without pay to make up for the crime for which you were convicted. You work for a government agency or some local non-profit organization, and you do not have any choice about where or what the job is. The judge decides the number of days and hours you must work. If you fail to work the required days and hours, you can be sent back to prison. You are also subject to random urinalysis testing.

Think about 12 months actual time in a medium-security correctional center.

What is the maximum number of hours of community service you would take to avoid serving *12* months actual time in prison? (Put an X on the line below to indicate the answer.)

0    250   500   750   1000   1500    2000   2500   3000   3500   4000   4500   5000

The X is equal to _____ hours of community service (write the number).

**(6). Day Reporting.** If you are sentenced to day reporting, you can stay home at night, but you must check in at a parole office every day. During the day you must have a job *or* you must go to some center in the community and be involved in activities all day. These activities might include working for no pay in the community, looking for a job, counseling, job training, and education programs. At the end of the day you get to go home. You may be *required* to work, and if you do you must check in *every day* during non-work hours. Failure to abide by the rules can result in you going back to prison. You are also subject to random urinalysis testing.

Think about 12 months actual time in a medium-security correctional center.

What is the maximum number of months of day reporting you would take to avoid serving *12* months actual time in prison? (Put an X on the line below to indicate the answer.)

0    4    8    12    16    20    24    28    32    36    40    44    48

_____

The X is equal to _____ months of day reporting (write the number).

(7). **Intensive Supervision Probation (ISP).** Intensive supervision is much more strict than regular probation. You do not go to prison and can live at home. However, the probation officer is checking up on you—sometimes everyday—and you are required to be in some kind of treatment program to improve yourself. All parts of your life, including what you do at home and at work are watched. Probation officers can come to your workplace or your home to check on you at any time of day or night. Sometimes you are required to report to the probation officer everyday on your own time. Failure to report to the officer or other violations can result in you going back to prison. You are also subject to random urinalysis testing.

Now think about 12 months actual time in a medium-security correctional center.

What is the maximum number of months of intensive supervision probation you would take to avoid serving *12* months actual time in prison? (Put an X on the line below to indicate the answer.)

0    2    4    6    8    10    12    14    16    18    20    22    24

---

The X is equal to _____ months of intensive supervision probation (write the number).

**(8). Intermittent Incarceration.** With this punishment, you must spend weekends or evenings in the county jail, which typically is much more unpleasant than prison. But, since you are not in prison, you can have a job and be involved with your family and community when you are not spending time in jail. However, failure to report to jail, or failure to pass a random urinalysis test can result in you returning to prison.

Now think about 12 months actual time in a medium-security correctional center.

What is the maximum number of months of intermittent incarceration you would take to avoid serving *12* months actual time in prison? (Put an X on the line below to indicate the answer.)

0    4    8    12    16    20    24    28    32    36    40    44    48

_____

The X is equal to _____ months of intermittent incarceration (write the number).

(9). **Halfway House**. A halfway house is a place where several people convicted of crimes live. There is no strict security like there is in prison, but there are firm rules that you must follow. Halfway houses have rehabilitative programs, and if your behavior improves you are treated better and given more freedom. Break the rules and you can be placed back in prison. As always, you are subject to random urinalysis and searches, and constant observation. You are not allowed to have visitors.

Now think about 12 months actual time in a medium-security correctional center.

What is the maximum number of months in a halfway house you would take to avoid serving *12* months actual time in prison? (Put an X on the line below to indicate the answer.)

0    4    8    12    16    20    24    28    32    36    40    44    48

_____

The X is equal to _____ months in a halfway house (write the number).

**(10). Day Fine.** A day fine is based on the amount of money you make each day. You are allowed to subtract some money for your rent, transportation, food, utilities, etc., but whatever is left over you have to pay as a day fine. For example, if you had $20 left each day after expenses, you day fine would be $20 for every day the judge says you have to pay. If the judge gives you a day fine of 90 days, and you day fine rate is $20, you would have to pay a total of $1800. Failure to pay your fines can result in you being sent back to prison.

Now think about 12 months actual time in a medium-security correctional center.

What is the maximum number of months of day fines you would take to avoid serving *12* months actual time in prison? (Put an X on the line below to indicate the answer.)

0    4    8    12    16    20    24    28    32    36    40    44    48

_____

The X is equal to _____ months of day fines (write the number).

# Appendix B

# Scales of Reasons to Avoid and Participate in Alternative Sanctions

## Reasons to Avoid Alternatives Scale

Respondents were asked to rate how important each of the following reasons were for avoiding alternative sanctions. Responses were then summed to create the index.

- Programs like those in this survey are too hard to complete.

- Program rules are too hard to follow.

- Parole and program officers are too hard on the program participants; they try to catch them and send them back to prison.

- Serving time in prison is easier than the alternatives offered by the Department of Corrections.

- If you fail to complete the alternative sanction, you end up back in prison.

- In general, living in prison is easier than living outside of prison.

- Inmates are abused by parole and probation officers who oversee the programs.

- Serving time in prison is less hassle because the programs have too many responsibilities.

# Reasons to Participate in Alternatives Scale

Respondents were asked to rate how important each of the following reasons were for participating in an alternative sanction. Responses were then summed to create the index.

- Alternatives offer a better lifestyle than prison.
- Alternatives allow the inmate to live outside the prison.
- Alternatives have a good reputation among the inmates.
- Alternatives are easier to complete than a prison term.
- Alternatives help you get out of prison sooner.

# Reasons to Avoid Prison Scale

Respondents were asked to rate how important each of the following reasons were for participating in an alternative sanction. Responses were then summed to create the index.

- Offender is being victimized by other inmates and is doing "hard time."
- Offender is serving his/her first time in prison.
- Correctional facility in which the offender is serving time is very strict on inmates.
- Offender is a woman.

# References

Akers, R. L., & C. Sellers. (2004). *Criminological theories: Introduction, evaluation, and application* (4th ed.). Los Angeles: Roxbury Publishing Company.

Albrecht, S. L., & Green, M. (1977). Attitudes toward the police and the larger attitudes complex: Implications for police-community relationships. *Criminology, 15,* 67–86.

Apospori, E. & Alpert, G. (1993). Research note: The role of differential experience with the criminal justice system in changes in perception of severity of legal sanctions over time. *Crime and Delinquency, 39,* 184–194.

Applegate, B. K., Cullen, F. T. & Fisher, B. S. (2002). Public views toward crime and correctional policies: Is there a gender gap? *Journal of Criminal Justice, 30,* 89–100.

Bae, I. (1991). A survey on public acceptance of restitution as an alternative to incarceration for property offenders in Hennepin County, Minnesota. Unpublished doctoral dissertation, University of Minnesota, Minneapolis, MN.

Bandura, A. 1977. *Social learning theory.* Englewood Cliffs, NJ: Prentice-Hall.

Becker, H. S. 1953. Becoming a marijuana user. *American Journal of Sociology 59,* 235–242.

Bennett, T., & Wright, R. (1984). *Burglars on burglary: Prevention and the offender.* Hampshire, England: Gower.

Bentham, J. (1998). Introduction to the principles of morals and legislation. In F. P. Williams & M. D. McShane (eds.) *Criminological Theories: Selected Case Readings.* Cincinnati, OH: Anderson.

Bohm, R. M. (1991). American death penalty opinion, 1936–1986: A critical examination of the Gallup polls. In R. M. Bohm (Ed.), *The Death Penalty in America: Current Research,* (pp. 113–145). Cincinnati, OH: Anderson.

Bonczar, T. (2003). *Prevalence of imprisonment in the U.S. population, 1974–2001.* Washington D.C.: U.S. Department of Justice, Bureau of Justice Statistics, NCJ 197976.

Bouffard, J. A. (2002). Methodological and theoretical implications of using subject-generated consequences in tests of rational choice theory. *Justice Quarterly 19*, 747–771.

Bouffard, J. A., & Piquero, A. (2008). Defiance theory and life course explanations of persistent offending. *Crime and Delinquency, April 8, 2008* (online first edition), 1–26. Retrieved April 14, 2009 from http://cad.sagepub.com. libproxy.eku.edu/cgi/rapidpdf/0011128707311642v1

Brandl, S. G., Frank, J., Worden, R.E., & Bynum, T.S. (1994). Global and specific attitudes toward the police: Disentangling the relationship. *Justice Quarterly, 11*, 119–134.

Brezina, T., & Piquero, A. R. (2003). Exploring the relationship between social and non-social reinforcement in the context of social learning theory. In R. Akers and G. Jensen (pp. 265–288) *Social learning theory and the explanation of crime*. New Brunswick, NJ: Transaction Publishers.

Brown, M. P., & Elrod, P. (1995). Electronic house arrest: An examination of citizen attitudes. *Crime and Delinquency, 41*, 332–346.

Burton, V. S., Ju, X., Dunaway, R. G., & Wolfe, N. T. (1991). The correctional orientation of Bermuda prison guards: An assessment of attitudes towards punishment and rehabilitation. *International Journal of Comparative and Applied Criminal Justice, 15*, 71–80.

Byrne, J. M. (1990). The future of intensive probation supervision and the new intermediate sanctions. *Crime & Delinquency, 36*, 6–41.

Byrne, J. A., Lurigio, A. J., & Petersilia, J. (1992). *Smart sentencing: The emergence of intermediate sanctions*. Thousand Oaks, CA: Sage.

Camp, C. G., & Camp, G. M. (1999). *The corrections yearbook 1999: Adult corrections*. Middletown, CT: Criminal Justice Institute, Inc.

Cao, L., Frank, J., & Cullen, F. T. (1996). Race, community context, and confidence in the police. *American Journal of Police, 15*, 3–22.

Carmichael, S., Langton, L., Pendell, G., Retizel, J. D., & Piquero, A. R. (2005). Do the experiential and deterrent effect operate differently across gender? *Journal of Criminal Justice, 33*, 267–276.

Clear, T. R. (1994). Harm in American penology: Offenders, victims, and their communities. Albany, NY: State University of New York Press.

Clear, T. R., & Hardyman, P. L. (1990). The new intensive supervision movement. *Crime & Delinquency, 36*, 42–60.

Clear, T., & Latessa, E. (1993). Probation officers roles in intensive supervision: Surveillance vs. treatment. *Justice Quarterly, 10* (3), 441–459.

Clear, T. R., & O'Leary, V. O. (1983). *Controlling the offender in the community*. Lexington, MA: Lexington Books.

Cole, G. F., Mahoney, B. F., Thornton, M., & Hanson, R. A. (1988). The use of fines by trial court judges. *Judicature, 71*(6), 325–333.

Cowan, J. L. (1969). The Gambler's Fallacy. *Philosophy and Phenomenological Research* 30; 238–251.

Crouch, B. M. (1993). Is incarceration really worse? Analysis of offenders' preferences for prison over probation. *Justice Quarterly*, 10, 67–88.

Cullen, F. T., Skovron, S. E., Scott, J. E., & Burton, V. S. (1990). Public support for correctional treatment: The tenacity of rehabilitative ideology. *Criminal Justice and Behavior, 17*, 6–18.

DataLinks, Inc. (1996). *Oklahoma judges and district attorneys on crime, punishment, and prisons.* Unpublished Technical Report prepared for the Oklahoma Department of Corrections.

Diamond, S., & Stalans, L. J. (1989). The myth in judicial leniency in sentencing. *Behavioral Sciences and the Law, 7*, 73–89.

Doleschal, E. (1982). Dangers of criminal justice reform. *Criminal Justice Abstracts, March*, 133–152.

Duffee, D. E. (1985). The interaction of organization and political constraints on community prerelease program development, pp. 62–78 in S. Stojkovic, J. Kofas, & D. Kalinich. *The administration and management of criminal justice organizations: A book of readings*, Prospect Heights, IL: Waveland Press.

Durham, A. M. III. (1994). *Crisis and reform: Current issues in American punishment.* Boston, MA: Little Brown and Company.

Durham, A. M., Ford, H. P., & Kinkade, P. T. (1996). Public support for the death penalty: Beyond Gallup. *Justice Quarterly, 13*, 705–736.

English, K., Crouch, J., & Pullen, P. (1989). *Attitudes towards crime: A survey of Colorado citizens and criminal justice officials.* Boulder, CO: Colorado Department of Public Safety, Division of Criminal Justice.

Fichter, M., & Veneziano C. (1988). *Criminal justice attitudes—Missouri.* Jefferson City, MO. Missouri Department of Corrections.

Finn, P. (1984). Judicial responses to prison overcrowding. *Judicature, 67*(7), 318–325.

Flanagan, T. J. & Longmire, D. R. (Eds.). (1996). *Americans view crime and justice: A national public opinion survey.* Thousand Oaks, CA: Sage Publications.

Fleisher, M. S. (1995). *Beggars and thieves: Lives of urban street criminals.* Madison, WI: University of Wisconsin Press.

Flory, C. M., May, D. C., Minor, K. I., & Wood, P. B. (2006). A comparison of punishment exchange rates between offenders under supervision and their supervising officers in Kentucky. *Journal of Criminal Justice, 34*(1), 39–50.

Frank, J., Brandl, S. G., Cullen, F. T., & Stichman, A. (1996). Reassessing the impact of race on citizens' attitudes toward the police: A research note. *Justice Quarterly, 13*, 321–334.

Fulton, B., Stichman, A., Travis, L., & Latessa, E. (1997). Moderating probation and parole officer attitudes to achieve desired outcomes. *The Prison Journal, 77*(3), 295–312.

Garland, D. (2001). The meaning of mass imprisonment. *Punishment and Society, 3*, 5–7.

Gibbons, D. C. (1992). *Society, crime, and criminal behavior (6th ed.)* Englewood Cliffs, NJ: Prentice Hall.

Gordon, J. A., Moriarty, L. J., & Grant, P. H. (2003). Juvenile correctional officers' perceived fear and risk of victimization. *Criminal Justice and Behavior, 30*(1), 62–84.

Grasmick, H., & Bursik, R. (1990). Conscience, significant others, and rational choice: Extending the deterrence model. *Law and Society Review, 24,* 837–861.

Greene, W. H. (2000). *Econometric analysis (4th ed.)* Upper Saddle River, NJ: Prentice-Hall.

Hagan, J., & Albonetti, C. (1982). Race, class, and the perceptions of criminal injustice in America. *American Journal of Sociology, 88*, 329–355.

Haghighi, B., & Lopez, A. (1998). Gender and perceptions of prisons and prisoners. *Journal of Criminal Justice, 26*(6), 453–464.

Hardyman, P. (1988). *No frills: A study of probation resources, activities and outcome.* Unpublished doctoral dissertation, Rutgers University, New Brunswick, NJ.

Hawkins, R., & Alpert, G. P. (1989). *American prison systems: Punishment and justice.* Englewood Cliffs, NJ: Prentice-Hall.

Henderson, M. L., Cullen, F. T., Cao, L., Browning, S. L., & Kopache, R. (1997). The impact of race on perceptions of criminal injustice. *Journal of Criminal Justice, 25*, 447–462.

Innes, C. A. (1993). Recent public opinion in the United States towards punishment and corrections. *The Prison Journal, 73*(2), 220–236.

Irwin, J., & Austin, J. (1997). *It's about time: America's imprisonment binge (2nd ed.).* Florence, KY: Wadsworth Publishing Company.

Jacoby, J. E., & Cullen, F. T. (1999). The structure of punishment norms: Applying the Rossi-Berk model. *Journal of Criminal Law and Criminology, 89,* 245–312.

John Doble Research Associates, Inc. (1995). *Crime and corrections: The views of the people of North Carolina.* Retrieved December 1, 2004, from http://www.doc.state.nc.us/NEWS/1996/96news/doblerep.htm

Keeney, R. L., & Raiffa, H. (1976). *Decision analysis with multiple conflicting objectives.* New York: Wiley.

Kifer, M., Hemmens, C., & Stohr, M. K. (2003). The goals of corrections: Perspectives from the lines. *Criminal Justice Review, 28* (1), 47–69.

King, R., Mauer, M., & Young, M. (2005). *Incarceration and crime: A complex relationship.* The Sentencing Project Report.

Klein, M. W. (1979). Deinstitutionalization and diversion of juvenile offenders: A litany of impediments. *Crime and Justice, 1,* 145–201

Klepper, S., & Nagin, D. 1989. The deterrent effects of perceived certainty and severity of punishment revisited. *Criminology 27,* 721–746.

Lemert, E. M. (1971). *Instead of court—Diversion in juvenile justice.* Washington D.C.: National Institute of Mental Health.

Lotzke, E., & Zeidenberg, J. (2005). *Tipping point: Maryland's overuse of incarceration and the impact on public safety.* Washington D.C.: Justice Policy Institute.

Lurigio, A.J. (1987). The perceptions and attitudes of judges and attorneys toward intensive probation supervision. *Federal Probation, 51*(1), 16–24.

Maguire, K. & Pastore, A.L. (Eds.). *Sourcebook of Criminal Justice Statistics* [Online]. Available: http://albany.edu/sourcebook/ [September, 2008].

Mauer, M. (1999). *Race to incarcerate.* New York: The New Press.

Mauer, M. (2001). The causes and consequences of prison growth in the United States. *Punishment and Society, 3,* 9–20.

Mauer, M., & Chesney-Lind, M. (2002). Invisible punishment: The collateral consequences of mass imprisonment. New York: The New Press.

May, D. C., Minor, K. I., Wood, P. B., & Mooney, J. L. (2004). Kentucky probationers' and parolees' perceptions of the severity of prison versus county jail and probation. *Kentucky Justice and Safety Research Bulletin: Justice and Safety Research Center, 6* (4), 1–9.

May, D. C., & Wood, P. B. (2005). What influences offenders' willingness to serve alternative sanctions? *The Prison Journal, 85*(2), 145–167.

May, D. C., Wood, P. B., Mooney, J. L., & Minor, K. I. (2005). Predicting offender-generated exchange rates: Implications for a theory of sentence severity. *Crime and Delinquency, 51*(3), 373–399.

McClelland, K. A., & Alpert, G. (1985). Factor analysis applied to magnitude estimates of punishment seriousness: Patterns of individual differences. *Journal of Quantitative Criminology, 1,* 307–318.

McCorkle, R. C. (1993). Research note: Punish and rehabilitate? Public attitudes towards six common crimes. *Crime and Delinquency, 39,* 240–252.

162 REFERENCES

Miller, J. L., Rossi, P. H., & Simpson, J. E. (1986). Perceptions of justice: Race and gender differences in judgments of appropriate prison sentences. *Law and Society Review, 20,* 313–334.

Moore, N. T. (2007). Continuing the reassessment of the punishment continuum: Judicial perceptions of the severity of alternative sanctions. Unpublished Master's Thesis submitted to Eastern Kentucky University, Richmond, Kentucky.

Moore, N. T., May, D. C., & Wood, P. B. (2008). Offenders, judges, and officers rate the relative severity of alternative sanctions compared to prison. *Journal of Offender Rehabilitation, 46*(3,4), 49–70.

Morash, M., & Schram, P. J. (2002). *The prison experience: Special issues of women in prison.* Prospect Heights, IL: Waveland Press.

Morris, N. & Tonry, M. (1990). *Between prison and probation: Intermediate punishments in a rational sentencing system.* New York: Oxford University Press.

Nagin, D. S. (1998). Criminal deterrence research at the outset of the twenty-first Century. *Crime and Justice, 23,* 51–91.

Nieuwbeerta, P., Nagin, D. S., & Blokland, A. A. Unpublished Manuscript. The relationship between first imprisonment and criminal career development: A matched samples comparison.

National Institute of Justice. (1995). *National assessment program: 1994 survey results.* Washington D.C.: U.S. Department of Justice Office of Justice Programs.

Paternoster, R. (1987). The deterrent effect of the perceived certainty and severity of punishment: A review of the evidence and issues. *Justice Quarterly, 4,* 173–217.

Paternoster, R., Brame, R., Mazerolle, P., & Piquero, A. (1998). Using the correct statistical test for the equality of regression coefficients. *Criminology, 36*(4), 859–866.

Paternoster, R., & Piquero, A. R. (1995). Reconceptualizing deterrence: An empirical test of personal and vicarious experiences. *Journal of Research in Crime and Delinquency 32,* 251–286.

Petersen, R. D., & Palumbo, D. J. (1997). The social construction of intermediate punishments. *The Prison Journal, 77,* 77–92.

Petersilia, J. (1990). When probation becomes more dreaded than prison. *Federal Probation, 54,* 23–27.

Petersilia, J. & Deschenes, E. P. (1994a). What punishes? Inmates rank the severity of prison vs. intermediate sanctions. *Federal Probation, 58,* 3–8.

Petersilia, J. & Deschenes, E. P. (1994b). Perceptions of punishment: Inmates and staff rank the severity of prison versus intermediate sanctions. *The Prison Journal, 74*, 306–328.

Petersilia, J., & Turner, S. (1990a). Comparing intensive and regular supervision for high-risk probationers: Early results from an experiment in California. *Crime & Delinquency, 36*, 87–111.

Petersilia, J., & Turner, S. (1990b). *Diverting prisoners to intensive probation: Results of an experiment in Oregon.* Santa Monica, CA: RAND Corporation, N–3186–NIJ.

Pettit, B., & Western, B. (2004). Mass imprisonment and the life course: Race and class inequality in U.S. incarceration. *American Sociological Review, 69*, 151–169.

Pew Center on the States. (2009). *One in 100: Behind bars in America, 2008.* Washington D.C.: Author.

Piquero, A., & Paternoster, R. (1998). An application of Stafford and Warr's reconceptualization of deterrence to drinking and driving. *Journal of Research in Crime and Delinquency, 35*, 3–39.

Piquero, A. R., & Pogarsky, G. (2002). Beyond Stafford and Warr's reconceptualization of deterrence: Personal and vicarious experiences, impulsivity, and offending behavior. *Journal of Research in Crime and Delinquency 39*, 153–186.

Pogarsky, G., & Piquero, A. R. (2003). Can punishment encourage offending? Investigating the 'resetting' effect. *Journal of Research in Crime and Delinquency 40*, 95–120.

Pogarsky, G., Piquero, A., & Paternoster, R. (2004). Modeling change in perceptions about sanction threats: The neglected linkage in deterrence theory. *Journal of Quantitative Criminology, 20*(4), 343–369.

Pollock, J. M. (2004). Prisons and prison life: Costs and consequences. Los Angeles, CA: Roxbury.

Pratt, T. C., Cullen, F. T., Blevins, K. R., Daigle, L. E., Madensen, T. D. (2006). The empirical status of deterrence theory: A meta-analysis. In *Taking Stock: The Status of Criminological Theory, volume 15*, edited by F. T. Cullen, J. P. Wright, & K. R. Blevins. New Brunswick, NJ: Transactions.

Reichel, P. (1998). *Comparative criminal justice systems.* Upper Saddle River, NJ: Prentice Hall.

Roberts, J. V., & Doob, A. N. (1989). Sentencing and public opinion: Taking false shadows for true substances. *Osgoode Hall Law Journal, 27*, 491–515.

Roberts, J. V., & Stalans L. J. (1997). *Public opinion, crime and criminal justice.* Boulder, CO: Westview Press, Harper Collins Publishers.

Roberts, J. V. & Stalans, L. J. (2000). *Public opinion, crime, and criminal justice.* Boulder, CO: Westview Press.

Ross, M., & F. Sicoly. (1979). Egocentric biases in availability and attribution. *Journal of Personality and Social Psychology, 37,* 322–336.

Rossi, P. H., Simpson, J. E., & Miller, J. L. (1985). Beyond crime seriousness: Fitting the punishment to the crime. *Journal of Quantitative Criminology, 1,* 59–90.

Santos, M. (2003). *About prison.* Florence, KY: Wadsworth.

Santos, M. (2006). *Inside: Life behind bars in America.* New York: St. Martin's Press.

Schur, E. (1973). Theoretical perspectives on deviance. *Contemporary Sociology, 2*(5), 487–489. Retrieved April 15, 2009, from Academic Search Premier database.

Sherman, L. W. (1993). Defiance, deterrence, and irrelevance: A theory of the criminal sanction. *Journal of Research in Crime and Delinquency 30,* 445–473.

Spelman, W. (1995). The severity of intermediate sanctions. *Journal of Research in Crime and Delinquency, 32,* 107–135.

Stafford, M. C., & Warr, M. (1993). A reconceptualization of general and specific deterrence. *Journal of Research in Crime and Delinquency 30,* 123–135.

Studt, E. (1978). *Surveillance and service to parole.* Washington, D.C.: U.S. Department of Justice, National Institute of Corrections.

Svenson, O. (1981). Are we all less risky and more skilled than our fellow drivers? *Acta Psychologica, 97,* 143–148.

Tonry, M. (1996). *Sentencing matters.* New York: Oxford University Press.

Topalli, V. (2005). When being good is bad: An expansion of neutralization theory. *Criminology, 43,* 797–835.

Topalli, V. (2006). The seductive nature of autotelic crime: How neutralization theory serves as a boundary condition for understanding hardcore street offending. *Sociological Inquiry, 76,* 475–501.

Tuch, S. A. & Weitzer, R. (1997). Racial differences in attitudes toward the police. *Public Opinion Quarterly, 61,* 642–663.

Tunnell, K. D. (1992). *Choosing crime: The criminal calculus of property offenders.* Chicago: Nelson-Hall Publishers.

Tunnell, K. D. (2000). *Living off crime.* Chicago: Burham Inc. Publishers.

Ulmer, J. (1997). Social worlds of sentencing: Court communities under sentencing guidelines. Albany, NY: State University of New York Press.

Vaughn, M. S. (1993). Listening to the experts: A national study of correctional administrators' responses to prison overcrowding. *Criminal Justice Review, 18,* 12–25.

Vieraitis, L. M., Kovandzic, T. V., & Marvell, T. B. (2007). The criminogenic effects of imprisonment: Evidence from state panel data, 1974–2002. *Criminology and Public Policy, 6*, 589–622.

von Hirsch, A. & Ashworth, A. (Eds.). (1992). *Principled sentencing*. Boston. Northeastern University Press.

von Hirsch, A., Wasik, M., & Greene, J. (1992). Scaling community punishments. In A. Von Hirsch & A. Ashworth, *Principled Sentencing* (pp. 368–388). Boston: Northeastern University Press.

Warr, M., Meier, R. F., & Erickson, M. L. (1983). Norms, theories of punishment, and publicly preferred penalties for crimes. *Sociological Quarterly, 24*, 75–91.

Weitzer, R. & Tuch, S. A. (1999). Race, class, and perceptions of discrimination by the police. *Crime and Delinquency, 45*, 494–507.

Wicharaya, T. (1995). Simple theory, hard reality: The impact of sentencing reforms on courts, prisons, and crime. Albany, NY: SUNY Press.

Williams, K. R., & Hawkins, R. (1986). Perceptual research on general deterrence: A critical review. *Law and Society Review, 20*(4), 545–572.

Williams, K. R., & Hawkins, R. (1989). The meaning of arrest for wife assault. *Criminology, 27*(1), 163–182.

Williams, A., May, D. C., & Wood, P. B. (2008). The lesser of two evils? A qualitative study of offenders' preferences for prison compared to alternative sanctions. *Journal of Offender Rehabilitation, 46*(3,4), 71–90.

Wood, P. B. & Grasmick, H.G. (1999). Toward the development of punishment equivalencies: Male and female inmates rate the severity of alternative sanctions compared to prison. *Justice Quarterly, 16*, 19–50.

Wood, P. B., & May, D. C. (2003). Race differences in perceptions of sanction severity: A comparison of prison with alternatives. *Justice Quarterly, 20*, 605–631.

Wood, P. B., Gove, W. R., Wilson, J. A., & Cochran, J. K. (1997). Nonsocial reinforcement and habitual criminal conduct: An extension of learning theory. *Criminology 35*, 335–366.

Wood, P. B., May, D. C., & Grasmick, H. G. (2005). Gender differences in the perceived severity of boot camp. *Journal of Offender Rehabilitation, (3,4)*, 153–175.

Wooldredge, J., & Gordon, J. (1997). Predicting the estimated use of alternatives to incarceration. *Journal of Quantitative Criminology, 13*(2), 121–142, doi:10.1007/BF02221305.

Wright, B., Avshalom Daspi, R. E., Moffitt, T. E., & Paternoster, R. (2004). Does the perceived risk of punishment deter criminally prone individual? Rational choice, self-control, and crime. *Journal of Research in Crime and Delinquency 41*, 180–213.

Wright, R. T., & Decker, S. C. (1994). *Burglars on the job: Streetlife and residential break-ins.* Northeastern University Press: Boston, MA.

# INDEX